W9-BRL-539

Surviving
DREADED
Conversations

Talk Through Any Difficult
Situation at Work

•

DONNA FLAGG

•

JERICHO PUBLIC LIBRARY

New York Chicago San Francisco Lisbon London Madrid Mexico City
Milan New Delhi San Juan Seoul Singapore Sydney Toronto

The _McGraw·Hill_ Companies

Library of Congress Cataloging-in-Publication Data

Flagg, Donna.
 Surviving dreaded conversations : talk through any difficult situation at work / by
 Donna Flagg.
   p.   cm.
 ISBN 978-0-07-163025-2
   1. Psychology, Industrial.   2. Language in the workplace.   3. Workplace
 environment.   I. Title.

 HF5548.8.F55   2009
 650.1'3—dc22   2009025625

Copyright © 2010 by The McGraw-Hill Companies, Inc. All rights reserved. Printed in the
United States of America. Except as permitted under the United States Copyright Act of
1976, no part of this publication may be reproduced or distributed in any form or by any
means, or stored in a database or retrieval system, without the prior written permission of
the publisher.

2 3 4 5 6 7 8 9 10 11 12 13 14 15 16 17 18 19 20 21 22   FGR/FGR   0 9

ISBN   978-0-07-163025-2
MHID   0-07-163025-2

McGraw-Hill books are available at special quantity discounts to use as premiums and
sales promotions or for use in corporate training programs. To contact a representative,
please visit the Contact Us pages at www.mhprofessional.com.

Contents

Part 3   The How

Acknowledgments

I love working, always have. I started as soon as I was able to find someone who would hire me, which initially was a family with kids in my neighborhood who needed a babysitter. Even though I was just a kid myself, I worked hard, feeding, bathing, diapering, and reading bedtime stories. Noting my industrious nature (and trouble in school—which is putting it mildly), my dad brought me into his office during the summers to "work." He put his secretary (in those days there were no "assistants," administrative, executive, or otherwise) in charge of "supervising" me. So I sat next to her like Liberace in front of a piano and ran my fingers up and down the keys of an IBM Selectric typewriter, enjoying the clickety-clack sounds that I was able to tap out with my fingertips. When I tired of that, I was assigned to organize paper clips, rubber bands, erasers, and staple refills in the office-supply closet, which I did earnestly and with focused intent. It was the first time—and only time, I'm sure—in the history of my dad's company that everything was lined up and coordinated by color.

When I was a little older, but not by much, I gave dance lessons to kids and taught aerobics to senior citizens. I know, it's an oxymoron; they sat in chairs for the whole class. I didn't care. I loved it. While I continued going to school, I managed to pick up an odd job here and an odd job there—and sometimes that meant *really* odd. For instance, I did clown makeup, worked events dressed up as Minnie Mouse and a James Bond Girl and pretended to be a mannequin on top of store displays for hours on end, although nothing beats the time that my parents put me to work capturing fleas off my two childhood Chihuahuas. And, yes, I got paid for that—*per flea*. What can I say? I was good at it. That, plus my dad was a real stickler for the value of work and its relationship to self-esteem.

By the time I was in high school, I had a normal job as a part-time employee at Bamberger's, which is now Macy's. That was the beginning of my official career track, which has since traveled down an extraordinary path—one that started at Chanel and ended at Goldman Sachs. That's when I started my own company, Krysalis.

But I must say that from the very beginning, regardless of what job I was in, I've wondered why people weren't naturally inclined to say what they wanted to or needed to say. See, I was unable to hold my thoughts and feelings in because doing so made me feel as though I might explode. So the words came flying out of my mouth, propelled by the pressure I felt inside. At first, I just assumed that everyone operated the same way. But I've come to learn that they don't.

Over the years I've said things to people that they weren't expecting and been accused of saying words that stung every bit as much as a square left hook to the jaw. No big surprise. I know this about myself. Even so, I still prepare for a return swing—I wince inside, close my eyes, and wait. But what continues to shock me time and time again is that instead of punches, I get hugs. Maybe not immediately, but eventually I do, and it has taught me the value of being forthcoming and forthright with people.

So when the opportunity arose for me to write this book on the subject of difficult conversations and the dread associated with them, I must say I was thrilled and decided to tailor it to the needs of today's workforce with an emphasis placed on communication as the most vital and powerful tool at our disposal. More important, it is intended to help people overcome the verbal constipation that holds them and their organizations back.

See, I was never convinced by the prevailing argument that difficult conversations were synonymous with conflict and confrontation. In fact, I think that they are two totally separate things that only sometimes overlap. For one, you can't learn to confront someone else effectively unless you've learned to confront yourself first, which tends to be biggest missing link in, and obstacle to, developing better communication skills.

Something else I struggle with is how easily difficult conversations have become confused with negotiating, when they also are two different animals. Let's face it, negotiating by its very nature creates an adversary and is typically about finding a means to one's own end. And while it may indeed be difficult to get one person to do what another wants, it also runs counter to creating genuine, heartfelt dialogue between individuals. So all of this focus has been directed toward teaching people how to create a win-win situation via difficult conversations, when ultimately the goal should be to learn how to say what you need to say and let others do the same.

So from babies to Minnie Mouse to Goldman Sachs and now at Krysalis, the sum total of my experience and whatever success has ensued is the sole result of the people whose paths I've crossed, the conversations we've had, and the effects they've had on me, respectively.

First is Patty Lee-Renert, my partner in Krysalis and, as I often say, "the other half of my brain." But more remarkably, she reads my mind, my gestures, and my handwriting when I have no idea what I am trying to say myself. If it hadn't been for Patty reading through every page and every word of this book, being there to tell me, "Donna, that makes no sense," there would be no book—or no company without Patty for that matter, either. She is my thinking partner.

My thanks also go to Joyce Avalon, my other partner, first boss, and friend who has believed in me unconditionally since the day she hired me at Chanel almost twenty years ago. She's brilliant, and I couldn't have asked for a better role model, teacher, and mentor.

And then there is John Aherne, my editor, whom I want to thank for finding me—and in this case "I" am equal to a needle in the proverbial haystack. How can I ever thank him enough for having the faith in me to pull this off in four and a half months? And to all the people on the McGraw-Hill team who supported the effort to bring this to fruition, I am grateful. Yes, it does take a village. . . .

Meanwhile, it's been said that it is not uncommon for people to have three careers over the course of their work lives. And while I think I am well into my fourth (if I'm counting correctly), it was Peter Bordes and Chris Travers whom I have to thank for essentially starting my fifth, in what has now become that of an author. They took a complete flyer on me and gave me a shot writing a column in their business publication, *Empire Magazine.* Without their enthusiasm for what I wrote and continued support of what I had to say, I'd not have had the opportunity to develop the confidence and skills I needed to sit down and write this book. And so, unknowingly I embarked on an industry of which I had no knowledge. But as luck would have it, I was graced by the goodness of a neighbor who happens to be a veteran in the world of publishing and book marketing. That said, I am so appreciative of David Horvath for his generosity, patience, and eagerness to help me navigate this new terrain. And, finally, I offer my heartfelt thanks to Judy Krusell, who played an integral role in my view on the world and who also taught me how to see the truth.

Most of all, I'd like to offer an extra-special thanks to the contributors who shared their wonderful stories of personal experience. Without them, this book would just not be that interesting. My deepest gratitude goes to them for participating in *Surviving Dreaded Conversations* and bringing these pages to "real" life.

Diane Bernard

Jamie Bernard

Sharon Blaivas, resume writer and founder of www .shakeupmyresume.com

Michele Bowbyes

Melinda Day-Harper, CEO, www.TZoneConsulting .com

Rich DiGirolamo, CAB, professional speaker and trainer with a diverse background in finance, sales, and leadership; www.richdigirolamo.com

Tom Douglas, Oakville, Canada, www.tomdouglas.type
pad.com

Rocco Greco

Jodi Katz

Leigh Kramer, president, www.helicoptermarketing.com

T. David Lee

Jolie Schoeffer

Pablo Solomon, artist and designer, www.pablosolomon
.com

Shirley Landis Van Scoyk, Realtor, Weichert, Realtors,
West Chester, Pennsylvania

Michele Wilcox, Sparks and Butterflies, www.sparksand
butterflies.com

In many ways my parents deserve the most credit of all
for putting up with me and my hairbrained ideas but, moreover, for advising me to follow my heart no matter what the
circumstances.

So, to *all* of the people who loved me enough to tell me
the truth, to all of the people who saw something in me
that I was unable to see myself, and to all of the people who
believed I could do things that I never thought I could do, I
thank you from the bottom of my heart.

*"Be who you are and say what you feel because those who mind
don't matter and those who matter don't mind."*

Part 1

The Why

1

From Dread to Said

There are, and always will be, things that we have to do whether we want to or not. For many, going to work is one of those things. Yet while liking work may be debatable for some and even unthinkable for others, not everyone hates his or her job. However, for most people in most workplaces, there are things that no one enjoys, such as having to have difficult conversations, communicate negative messages, and deliver bad news. These are the tête-à-têtes that come with the territory of working in today's workforce that we've learned to dread with every fiber of our being. They keep us up at night worrying because we know we need to have them. We have no choice. Meanwhile, we put them off for as long as we can. We cringe at the thought of having to utter the words that we know must be said and wonder how we will ever muster up the courage to look someone in the eye and "tell 'em like it is." We *do not* want to do it. But there is no way out.

It could be a manager who has to inform an employee that he no longer has a job or a sales executive who has to deliver the news to senior management that she angered a client and, as a result, lost the company its biggest account. But it could also be something much smaller in magnitude, for there are plenty of less significant and more mundane conversations that happen every day which are capable of creating as much dread as "the big ones." For example, I recently had someone tell me that he would rather die than tell his coworkers that their lunches were rotting in the refrigerator. It was so simple—he just wanted them to toss out their moldy sandwiches. But he remained silent because he froze somewhere in between not knowing what to say and not knowing how to say it.

If you think about it, though, this makes perfect sense. Lots of people struggle with how to assemble words in a way that make negative sounding messages sound, well . . . not so negative. So, naturally, if people are afraid to say what they think and feel because they don't know how in the first place, then of course it stands to reason that they would shy away from the awkwardness that comes from trying something new and unfamiliar. But the problem with choosing silence over words is that you deprive yourself of an opportunity to learn. So then the question becomes "How will you learn if you don't practice, and how will you practice if you are paralyzed by fear?" Particularly within work environments where individuals are measured, rewarded, and potentially penalized for every little thing they do, it is understandable that employees would be less apt to take the risk and try merely in the name of honing their skills. So the cycle just goes round and round, while we go nowhere.

The bigger problem, however, is that long before we get into the workforce, life simply has not provided us with sufficient opportunities to practice telling people the things that they do not want to hear. Well, actually, it does, but for some reason our society dictates that those opportunities should be ignored because somewhere along the line *someone* decided that *the truth hurts* more than a lie. It's beyond ridiculous, but it stuck. And now, like it or not, we're left to deal with dodging, procrastinating, sugarcoating, eschewing, soft-pedaling, and, yes, dreading conversations that should otherwise be straightforward and easy to have.

The point is that by holding back what we have to say, we hold ourselves, our relationships, and our organizations back, too. Words need to move. Words need to flow. If we allow ourselves to be verbally constipated by a belief that speaking the truth is bad, then bad is what we will indeed get. But it doesn't have to be.

Learning a New Language

Learning to wrap words around difficult messages is no harder than learning a new language. In fact, it's easier because you don't have to start from scratch. Rather, you just need to adapt the language you already know and use it differently. Think of it this way. Your brain and your mouth are your hardware. These are the operational components that must work together in order to code and generate language. Then you have your thoughts and words that make up the software, or application, which converts the language into a process of communication. And lastly is the inclusion of the human voice and heart, which together bring emotion into the discussion. This is perhaps the hardest and most complex part about carrying out a difficult conversation successfully, because emotions running high are what most often deteriorate the integrity of a conversation. However, emotion is also the *only* thing that separates us as humans from machines. So having no emotion doesn't work either because a lack of feelings and a robotic, mechanical attitude will come across as cold, heartless, and uncaring.

All told, like muscles that get stronger and bodies that become more agile when they are "activated," verbal dexterity and mastery with words can be cultivated when individual hardware is coordinated, software is exercised, and emotions are balanced. In a way, it is similar to attaining physical fitness, but instead, here it is about training yourself to be healthy in conversations so the dread doesn't get the best of you and the chances for a positive outcome are greatly increased.

This assumes, however, that your perception of what qualifies as positive is in perspective. If, for example, you are afraid of what another person's reaction will be, or are vested in the outcome ahead of time, chances are that you will experience higher levels of anxiety than those who aren't afraid or vested in anything when it comes to having to broach an unpleasant subject with a coworker. Why? Because fear of something outside yourself that you cannot control creates the kind of stress that will paralyze you and the conversation.

Frankly, I think that an excessive amount of focus has been placed on the "other person" in dealing with difficult conversations, which has turned the topic into one that is almost exclusively limited to conflict and confrontation. But that's wrong. To assume that disagreement is what makes a conversation difficult is to speak only to those people who fear clashing with another and want to avoid a dispute at any cost. Yet in truth, there are plenty of people who not only like conflict, but thrive on it. So it is not sufficient to link dread with conflict because while conflict stimulates some and argument intrigues others, dread is dread for everyone. In other words, it doesn't matter how another person reacts because these conversations are not dependent on the behavior of someone else. Rather, the success or failure depends on you.

The reality is that the *really* tough and most dreaded conversations have more to do with the inherent intrapersonal challenges that come with having to say something that is awkward, uncomfortable, unpleasant, potentially hurtful, and just plain yucky than they do with interpersonal discord. So, while conflict in difficult conversations is typically positioned as a game in resolution and the ability to influence another person, surviving dreaded conversations, for the purpose of this book, is about resolving and influencing *yourself.*

Trial by Fire

It's been the result of having spent many years in business and experiencing plenty of uncomfortable, and even painful, conversations along the way that I came to the conclusion that if you worry about what *might* happen or what someone *might* do or say, you create the kind of barrier that can be difficult, if not impossible, to overcome. Instead, if you concentrate on what *needs* to be said and figure out the best way to say it for *you*, then not only can you survive what seems an insurmountable task, but you can actually do it well.

Specifically, this view came into focus for me during one of the most horrifying moments of my career. Here's what happened. I worked for a cosmetics company managing a territory of stores up and down the East Coast. My boss informed my West and Central counterparts and me that we were to promote our top producers who sold our products for our retail partners in key markets around the country. This meant removing them from the stores' hourly payrolls and creating salaried positions with us. There was one stipulation, however. Before we could move everyone into the higher-level, higher-paying jobs, each person had to find his or her own replacement. So that's what they did, because remember, they were our best and brightest.

After about four weeks had passed, we got another call. This time it was from the CFO. Apparently he'd miscalculated the cost of his plan. We were then instructed to go back through our territories and tell the superstars whom we'd handpicked, promoted, and showered with accolades that we had made a mistake. Now, not only were we "unpromoting" them, but we—correction, *I*—had to tell them that they had done such a good job replacing themselves and we had done such a poor job budgeting that we had nowhere for them to go. Oh, my gosh—talk about dread. I was stupefied. We all were. There was absolutely no way I could sit down at the same table where I'd praised and rewarded these people only to fire them a mere few weeks later. But I had to do it. I had no choice. Uggghhh. I was sick. So, so sick. In retrospect, though, I did learn something important about the ins and outs of getting through a dreaded conversation.

Since I basically had to say the same thing six times, I saw that while reactions varied from anger, hate, hysteria, betrayal, tears, and silence to crippling shock, the message I delivered remained the same. What had to be said, had to be said regardless of what happened next. All I could do was (a) tell them what happened and (b) explain how I felt. What also became very clear with each grueling round was that I got better and better and it got easier and easier. So I bit the bullet, dropped the bomb, and then sat as still as I could, holding on to the arms of my chair, waiting for the emotional storms to pass.

Needless to say, the positive and productive relationships that I'd cultivated with my direct reports were blown to smithereens in an instant. I went from being their well-liked boss to the worst one they ever had. The trust was gone. Their respect for me was gone. And everything we'd worked to build together as a team was gone. They hated me.

Now, I realize that everything about the situation I've described is exactly why conversations of this nature are so dreadful. Understandably so. And it was. I will say, though, that this was also the one on which I cut my teeth because, like batting with a donut on the end of a bat, everything that came after was easy in comparison. But what makes this story interesting, beyond what it taught me, is that I received a letter from one of those employees ten years after the fact. It was from the one who took it the hardest and despised me the most, or so I thought at the time. I know, like a parent, we're not supposed to have favorites, but I did and she was one of mine. A most talented, gifted, and creative woman, I remember feeling particularly nauseated having to let her go.

The letter came in a box with something else nestled in burgundy tissue inside. Along with a most touching, heartfelt letter, there was a doll that she'd made and named Donna, after me. Admittedly, at first my partner, Patty, and I assumed it had to be a voodoo doll. We tossed the box and rummaged through the tissue searching for long straight pins that we were sure had to be in there. After all, when this employee and I had that final conversation, she had refused to speak to me. Did I mention how terrible I felt? Anyway, it turns out that "Donna" was among a collection of handmade dolls made in honor of women whom my former employee admired. She described her recollection of me as a mentor. Not a monster. She didn't hate me after all. In fact, it was quite the opposite. I couldn't believe it.

Looking back I realize that there were things I did and said of which I was totally unaware at the time but that have proven to be effective—things like getting to the point but not rushing, allowing the humanistic part of me to show through without getting too personal and blaming no one else for what I had to say. I made no excuses. Today, albeit years later, I also believe that these are the reasons why this story ended on such a positive note.

On this, I have one last point with regard to timing. If you are the one with a dreaded conversation before you and it is serious in nature, as I was in the example above, be sure that you take responsibility for it and start the dialogue yourself. Do *not* have the person on whom you need to land the bad news be the one to approach you. Otherwise you lose the opportunity to set up the conversation properly, which is the single most important thing because it sets the tone for what follows. Translation: the more you avoid it and procrastinate, the more you chip away at your chances for success and increase the odds that your conversation won't go well.

On the other hand, sometimes you may dread talking with someone about something, but the matter is not pressing, the need to discuss it is not imminent, and it is not a do-or-die situation. Then it can pay to wait. A thoughtful pause may serve as a useful strategy if you want to let the discussion come up naturally, when a conversation can then organically unfold. It's a judgment call, but either way, you'll no doubt learn as you go.

Speaking of learning as you go, this book is not intended to prepare you for a battle, nor is its aim to analyze difficult conversations to death. No, not by a long shot. Rather, this book is to show you how to "get it out" in place of trying to "work it out." It's important to know, however, that there can be no success without practice. So, if you are not willing to move beyond the thinking level and start doing, then the best advice I have before you go any further is to *return this book and get a refund!* It will not help you on a cognitive level alone. Surviving dreaded conversations is dependent upon taking action as well.

2

Healthy Heads, Healthy Hearts, Healthy Words

As I embarked on the process of writing this book and began talking with people about what types of conversations they dreaded and why, I was overwhelmed by the pattern that emerged. It was surprising, at least to me, how many said that they didn't like to discuss anything "negative." But what was outright shocking were the things that they considered too taboo, off-limits, or forbidden to talk about. For example, one man was unable to tell his assistant that complaints were coming in from clients about her bad attitude. Another person told me he couldn't approach one of his direct reports with questions about a dubious charge on an expense report. Someone even said that she couldn't ask his boss to stop yelling at her in meetings. And there were more. One man couldn't tell his office mate that she spit all over him when she talked, and a manager did not have the courage to request that her male colleague refrain from staring at her breasts when she spoke to him.

That's when I realized that dread is not something as over-arching or generic as I thought, but rather, and more specifically, it is an emotion tied directly to individual perceptions of negativity. Maybe so, but I happen to come at this from a completely different angle. Mainly, I don't believe that telling someone what you think or how you feel is negative in any way. In fact, on the contrary, I think it's extremely positive. Crucial even. Therefore, in my mind's eye what makes or breaks the ease with which a dreaded conversation is possible rests somewhere between the personal choices we make and the individual mind-set we bring to it.

Now, we've already established that it's not easy to face someone and say something that we *know* he or she is not going to want to hear and that for many, like those individuals in the examples just given, it's impossible. However, for as long as communication continues to be understood along this continuum as being something either good *or* bad, there is little room in the middle for a balanced alternative where neutral and healthy exchanges of *all* sorts can take place. Of course, no one expects anyone to enjoy delivering bad news or hurting someone else's feelings. That's a given. But there are ways to say things that don't have to inflict pain. So, if you can accept that the hardest conversations will never feel great, but also that they don't have to be devastating either, you can begin to form a healthy approach to communicating with others by freeing your words and using them to create a language that works best for you.

This starts by making some choices—that is, choices about your thoughts, your feelings, and your words. And to ensure that your choices work for and not against you, you'll need to acquaint yourself with your ego and be willing to look at its role in your life. Otherwise, without an understanding of how ego colors and shades our realities, all hope of successfully linking what we think to what we feel to what we say is lost because egos interfere with the clarity of hearts and minds and distort everything they touch. By their very nature, egos exist to defend against a perceptual reality informed and skewed by events of the past that may or may not be relevant in, or representative of, the present. So it matters more than anything that they take their appropriate place in history and leave their "hosts" alone and free to function in the here and now.

Letting Go fo Your Ego

First, in order to effectively manage your ego it is necessary to acknowledge the interdependent relationship between healthy people and healthy conversations, because in the end, they are inextricably linked. But health isn't reflected in the body alone. Egos have to be fit, too. Irrespective of firm muscles and strong bones, if people aren't intrinsically healthy—in heart, mind, *and* psyche, too—the conversations between them can't and won't be either. This is why it is well worth the short-term effort of "working out" your ego now to prepare for the long-term gains associated with an improved ability to communicate with others.

That being the case, I wish I could say that whipping an ego into shape was as concrete and clear-cut a task as going to the gym and eating right. Unfortunately, it's not. It's more elusive than that. But make no mistake. A noxious ego is as harmful to a person's growth both professionally and personally as weak, sickly, undeveloped, and atrophied muscles are to a body. In fact, if ignored, your ego will suffocate you inside its own warped reality the same way a body uncared for will eventually collapse. You won't grow or learn or become stronger *on the inside*, which is where it counts if you truly want to develop your skills and become a stronger, more satisfied employee, person, and communicator.

It's amazing actually. We all know and recognize the ego in a room when it's someone else's, and typically we don't like it. Sometimes we even detest it. It's that *thing* in people that requires attention, sees only itself, is short on compassion, takes things personally, is defensive, sucks the air out of the room, and/or blames others for its failures. Yet when it comes to our own ego, we don't see, feel, or hear it. Mysterious? It is. And while it is important to admit that the coexistence between a conscious self and an unconscious ego is not only universal but the meaning of being human itself, it is not sufficient to stop there. Remember, your ego hides only from you. Not others. So it's up to you to *see* it in all its glory along with what it's capable of. When you realize how it interferes with your ability to communicate, chances are good that you are going to want to send it packing and bid it farewell. But beware! It won't go willingly or easily. The little buggers have got some chops.

For this, I offer my own homespun explanation. Admittedly, it's not very technical—or Freudian, for that matter. Nonetheless, in a nutshell, egos are old but young, and the person to whom they belong is caught somewhere in the middle. They're old because their births date back to a time early in life when someone else made them/us feel insecure, rejected, inadequate, threatened, or invisible. Something in us, at the time and thereafter, assumed that the information coming from the outside world was "right," whether it was or not. This in turn automatically triggered a defense intended to insulate us from the pain of feeling disapproved of, and the ego set out on a mission to prove untrue whatever ensuing beliefs resulted. The more this situation repeated itself, the thicker the protective callus became, and with that, each layer made it harder and harder to see and feel (and later say) what was underneath.

Conversely, egos are young, too, because they're stuck there, frozen in time within us, and unable to mature normally through the natural stages of life. They never quit. They never die. They never advance. They never let go. At least not on their own they don't. They require intervention, because left to their own devices, they are perfectly happy running in the background of our minds the same way virus protection software goes nonstop for as long as a computer is on. Yet unlike the software that we use to keep us safe, our egos are no longer protecting us like they were when they came into being and we needed them to absorb the sorrow of childhood that we were too young to understand, process, and incorporate. No. In adulthood, they *become* the virus.

All told, we manage to survive childhood, get through puberty, and enter adulthood appearing to have grown on the outside. Yet on the inside, the ego is still fighting the same old battle based on a set of beliefs that by now are completely irrelevant and against threats that aren't even there. It's that simple. On its own, the ego won't budge. So we go to work and it comes with us only to get in the way by inserting the mind, heart, and communication ability of a wounded child into the daily course of doing business.

But that's a huge problem because when something triggers the ego, the symbiosis of the organization and people in it is thrown totally out of whack, to the detriment of everyone and everything *but* the ego. Consequently, you and the people around you suddenly become subjected to the pain of your childhood, which in the work setting is taken entirely out of context. Therefore, in that moment you divide the workplace into a past that conflicts with the present and a fantasy that contradicts reality. What a mess.

In other words, maybe you know that you should be fair and equitable with people; in fact, you may even want to consciously do the right thing. And most of the time, you probably do. But when a situation arises that evokes a memory and sparks the negative or insecure feelings you've buried about *yourself*, your ego automatically activates *itself.* So there you are, behaving in a manner that is incongruent, and perhaps even diametrically opposed, to the way you think you are acting and the way you perceive yourself to be.

See, egos are not able to distinguish between "then" and "now." You have to do that for them. But in the meantime, when they feel threatened they continue responding with the same behaviors learned long ago. Ultimately, this then manages to turn your positive attitudes of today into negative and destructive remnants of yesterday. That's not good. Not now. Not at work. Not when you're trying to communicate. For example, a desire to be generous could turn into just the opposite if the ego is allowed to wedge itself into the situation. Fairness can become biased. Celebrating shared success can be replaced with hogging the limelight. Truthfulness can suddenly morph into a lie. Now multiply that by all the people in an organization and imagine the complete and utter mayhem that is bound to ensue. It's hard, if not impossible, to tell in what era, in what place, and with whom you are actually interacting when people's egos bring these untenable figments forward from a land of distant, distorted events.

However, it is also important to point out that all of this psychological complexity is what it means to be human as well. Ego is a challenge to humanity, one that I suspect has been with us since the beginning of time. And if you don't have to wrestle with your own, chances are you'll have to deal with someone else's at some point along the way.

All that said, my intent here is not to conduct a childhood analysis. Not by any stretch. It's pointless as far as the workplace is concerned. Plus there is a plethora of resources available for those who want to dive into their pasts and dig into their souls to better understand themselves. What we need instead is a way to go to work every day, communicate better, survive the unbearable conversations, and create the kind of success that makes us feel happy. To that end, all we need to bring to the fore are the basic links that connect then to now so that we can see the past for what it is, learn to manage it, and move on. To achieve that is acquire an understanding of how the ego evolves. I like to call it "EGOlution," which just means looking at how the ego develops so that we can learn to work with it constructively in the realm of workplace communications.

Ego's Life Story

There are two different but very important ways to evaluate ego. People often say to me, "Ego is good. We need it."

And I say back, "That depends." It's true that at its heart, the core function of ego is to protect. And yes, we need protection from bad things at all stages of life. But it's what ego deems as a threat and what it defends against that makes it either troublesome or not. A good ego is not disfigured and is able to protect against bad egos. Conversely, a bad ego creates and re-creates bad things to keep the person to whom it belongs scared. Then that way, it feels important and you don't. Here's how it worked . . .

1. **Born to Run.** Back in the day you took a hit and it landed in a place that is impossible for a child to locate, let alone be conscious of or understand. Unlike stubbing a toe and watching it bleed or burning a hand and witnessing the formation of a blister, injuries to the heart, soul, psyche, and self-esteem are elusive but nonetheless hurt like hell. So down you went, but your ego got up instead.

2. **The Clot Thickens.** Not only was that the beginning of a protective outer shell, wrapping itself around the outside of you like an oyster covering a pearl, but its hardness and thickness increased at a rate that was dependent on the frequency and severity of each subsequent blow. So the more you suffered and were unable to process it, the stronger and more robust your ego had to become in order to ward off the pain. But unfortunately, in exchange for that protection the ego prohibited the healthy development of your self-esteem. So in the end, it is a costly swap that turns into a full-blown self-fulfilling prophecy. As your ego greased its wheels, it increasingly took control, and you became more and more defensive as a person struggling to conceal scars that you believed would reveal some sort of horrible secret.

3. **Smoke and Mirrors.** Gradually as your ego became more and more integrated into your "self," it stopped operating offensively and began working defensively. Then one day, you're reacting to anyone or anything that reminds you of how you felt at the time of the original injuries, regardless of their accuracy now. The problem with this is that it leaves you responding to, and suffering from, memories of situations and feelings rather than being open to experience your current reality as it *actually* is now.

4. **Negativity Personified.** With its persistent voice and determination to implicate the past, ego's existence becomes dependent on you feeling insecure and/or bad about yourself, because remember, its fundamental enactment was to be a shock absorber for whatever emotional pain came your way. But those times are over and we're adults. So as long as an ego is allowed to spin everyday scenarios into negative versions of something learned years ago, it sustains its purpose of *being*, and you are generating and regenerating negative thoughts and feelings about yourself. This not only makes it hard to have healthy, lucid, and adult conversations at work, but it is also what fuels and feeds your personal perceptions of negativity.

5. **Access Denied.** Should it be the case that you decide to rely more on the protective, warped ego for your identity than on whom you really are underneath, you essentially mummify and therefore preserve all those feelings of insecurity that the ego was born to defend against in the first place. But then you're also closed off from yourself and others. And if you attempt to operate at work in a "no access" mode on the human level and try to have a difficult conversation, peo-

ple will sense it and think you are cold, fake, and unfeeling. That does not bode well for your effectiveness in conversation, difficult or not, nor will it help with others' receptivity toward you.

6. **From Friend to Foe.** Suddenly, somehow without you knowing it, your ego who was once your best friend is now your greatest enemy and as a result, you've become operational in an alternative version of yourself. You're not *really* "you," yet informed by your ego, you're acting the only way you know how.

7. **The Turning Point.** The choice is yours. It will be up to you to figure out your own crossroads to determine if, and at what point, your ego is taking you backward and no longer forward.

8. **Just Say No.** This is where the hardest conversation of all begins because it requires a truth so honest, an openness so unfettered, courage so unwavering, and a willingness to learn that is so unconditional, your ego can't survive it. Why? Because egos are the antithesis of all those things. They are clouded, afraid, closed, and stubborn. Remember, they have the will of a child trapped inside. So be prepared. Egos do *not* like to being told to hit the road. Those are the words of rejection your ego has been fighting against and denying your whole life. When you admit that your ego is useless and that you no longer need it, it won't agree. You'll have to become as persistent with it as it has been with you and stay focused on your objective. You have to manage the force that it has become and reverse the embedded effects if you want to clear the barrier that your ego creates to having open, healthy, and

fear-free conversations. The point being, you're in control as soon as you take the steering wheel away from your ego.

By changing the direction of your own internal compass and turning your ego on its head, you accomplish a few things that prepare and equip you for the simplest to the most complicated dreaded conversations at work and otherwise. For starters, *negative* loses its negativity, the truth goes from being bad to good, fear turns into freedom, and insecurity shifts to confidence. And the big picture is that these conversations become easier due to an acquired mastery because the process itself starts from a new point of clarity with you having fundamentally changed the lens through which you see the world. It is no small feat. If it were, the world, including our workplaces, would look quite different. We would not be mired in so much drama or bogged down by other people's fears that their own deficiencies might be revealed. Instead, we would know supportive environments filled with confident people who are interested in creating positive healthy space for themselves and others.

The process of understanding yourself by way of your ego is a process made of the same critical components that enable people to communicate effectively during the most difficult of circumstances with others. Why? Because you have to talk honestly with yourself first, which is the most important conversation of all. The added benefit is that when you learn from the inside out, you bring a kind of authenticity that very few people have.

Application: A Meeting with Your Ego

Write yourself a letter.

1. Use your nondominant hand and imagine yourself as a child. Write an apology to him or her.
2. Split a piece of paper into two columns. On the left side write your name, and on the right side write "Ego." Start a conversation between you and your ego on the left-hand side of the paper with the words "What did I need you for?" On the right-hand side, answer the question from your ego's point of view. Bounce from side to side building responses from both perspectives. When you are done, ask one last question of your ego: "What have you done for me lately?"
3. Read the conversation that transpired back to yourself. Look at the ego's voice and figure out whom it sounds like. You'll be surprised because it's not you.

3

Personalities and Feelings

Typically, the biggest problem for people confronted with a difficult conversation in the workplace is that they have to face the other person—*in person*. We've all been mortified at one time or another by examples of how news went out over the wires that clearly would have been easier on the recipient(s) had the information been communicated face-to-face. Maybe a manager gave negative performance feedback to an employee in an e-mail or a coworker gave a colleague a piece of his or her mind on voice mail. Heck, maybe an investment adviser sat back and did nothing to notify his clients that their 401(k)s had plummeted when the market crashed because he figured he'd let the press take care of it. RadioShack even fired roughly four hundred employees using e-mail in lieu of verbally informing them that they no longer had jobs. Now that was cold. What's baffling, though, is that these people who make the decision to avoid a personal conversation under difficult circumstances know it's bad, cowardly, and hurtful to others as much as they know they would not like it if the same were done to them. So one has to ask, "Why go that route?" It makes no sense. That is, unless we bring ego back into the fold, which is what we are going to do, because no matter how you slice it, it *is* the root of all dysfunction, which means it is also what makes so many hard conversations harder.

Remember, egos distort reality no matter which side of the proverbial table they're on. So whether it is yours or someone else's, it has the potential to wreak havoc and disrupt the normal and healthy flow of a conversation. Oddly enough, though, difficult conversations tend to be harder on the bearer of bad news, which I find counterintuitive, because the person receiving the information is technically the one who should be experiencing the most pain. But that's not the case. The person who has to have the conversation typically experiences more anxiety than the one receiving it. Go figure.

While I'm convinced that this common trepidation relates primarily to fear of the other person's outward reaction, I also think dreading these conversations has to do with looking someone in the eyes and having to process what he or she is "saying" silently. Let's face it, a lot of communicating happens through the eyes. But when the expression in human eyes contradicts the words coming out of one's mouth, adding another layer of strain, dissonance, and uncertainty is added to the discussion. A good example of this is when someone looks hurt and even appears to be on the verge of tears, all the while saying, "I'm fine." That's confusing. Fearing one reaction is bad enough, but then worrying about the duality of what is said versus what is not said only makes these conversations harder to manage and interpret accurately, thereby making a precarious situation more unstable and a tenuous situation worse.

Going Beyond Personality Types

Once the verbal and nonverbal discrepancies have been reconciled, or at least acknowledged, the next thing we need to do is disengage from the idea that conflict is the default cause for dread in difficult conversations and, moreover, that the nature of that conflict is somehow attributable to differences in personality "types." That's crazy thinking. All "typing" does is box people into theoretical constraints that are as telling of someone's behavior as a horoscope is able to predict one's day. Yet there have long been inferences and assertions that personal incompatibility *between* people was the reason for friction and lack of mutual understanding when trouble arose in the professional communication process. Furthermore, it was assumed that an effort to define, and then label, someone else's traits would be solution enough to maneuver their dissimilarities during communication challenges. This isn't true. Individual personalities are not only irrelevant, but the differences among them are what make communication rich and valuable—not cumbersome and certainly not impossible. What makes difficult conversations difficult is the ego, *period*. Personality does not present the obstacle that many want to make it when it comes to effectively communicating. It's that little bogeyman *beneath* one's personality that you need to keep your eye on and worry about.

And so we find ourselves right back where we started, at this basic idea of *human versus ego*, wherein people tend to present one person to the world on the outside while hiding another, more vulnerable one on the inside. It's anyone's guess where the demarcation line is drawn for each individual, but essentially it means that a person could reveal his or her *other* self with no notice and catch the unwitting bystander completely by surprise. No wonder why people are afraid to face other people sometimes. There's nothing scarier than something that hides behind what we can see and that is capable of jumping out at any moment. Think about it for a second: There were Jason and Freddy Krueger. And then, of course, we had Jaws, too. Ego works the same way and can have as debilitating an effect as any other creature that lurks in the shadows. The point is that you can't possibly be effective in a situation that operates from a foundation of fear, which is exactly what the unpredictability of ego creates. So understood this way, it's no wonder why people walk into these conversations feeling so much dread. Who wouldn't? Insecurity and uncertainty make an awful platform for healthy dialogue specifically and human interaction in general. Admittedly, to include the ego is to make everything sound schizophrenic. That's because it is. In fact, that's exactly what ego is—a split personality with a strong identity of its own, complete with a voice and an agenda. Egos split people in two, especially during stressful situations such as a difficult conversation, which is highly likely to trigger the very defense mechanism that sent the ego running to the rescue in the first place. Coupled with the fact that an ego is *not* rational and can quickly make a situation feel out of control, it's perfectly reasonable that these unexpected, uninvited, unfledged guests would raise legitimate concerns for anyone. But not to worry—all you need to do to render them impotent is be prepared for the time when they rear their ugly heads.

In the next several pages, you'll see how to look for and identify ego's personas. We call the process the "Ego Patrol."

Once you learn to recognize the ego's attributes in others the way you learned to see your own in yourself earlier in Chapter 2, you'll be amazed at how easy it is to keep a conversation on track. No longer do you need to be bound to the fear associated with having to deal with someone else's reaction/ego, because when you understand how to handle its emergence and know what to say to manage it, you'll have control. Remember, ego only takes the power over you that you allow it to have. If you refuse, there is then nothing to be afraid of.

Egoist/Egoista 1: The Ticking Time Bombs

Think Tasmanian devil. These folks are volatile, inconsistent, and unpredictable. They fly off the handle easily and feel empowered by making others walk on eggshells. They stifle free dialogue by shutting other people down, and they kill the possibility of having productive conversations by breeding insecurity in their relationships.

- The **Tyrant** rants and raves and makes no sense.
- The **Ogre** is grumpy and unpleasant and snaps for no reason.
- The **Bully** derives pleasure from pushing other people around.
- The **Loose Cannon** is quiet and pent up but abusive when set off.

How to Deal

Weather the storm. Remain calm no matter what. Do not feed the monster or it will eat you alive. If you ever heard a story about what to do should you find yourself face-to-face with a lion in the wilderness, you know your only chance at survival is to stare it down, eye-to-eye, and remain still until it is convinced by your lack of fear that you are not the perfect prey.

What to Say

"Whoa, hold on." For starters, ask the Ticking Time Bomb to stop. Request that he or she refrain from snapping, bullying, abusing, ranting, raving, etc. . . . State that you don't do well under attack and that you'd like the conversation to progress in a mutually respectful way. Depending on the relationship, if it's appropriate, you can also point out that this person seems a bit more on edge than usual and ask if there is anything you can do to help. This softens the demon. And mostly, don't make it harder than it has to be. On many occasions, I have simply said to people who felt the need to push me around, "Please don't bully me. I don't like it." It works!

Egoist/Egoista 2: The Centers of the Universe

These people have a bad case of me, me, me myopia. They only see themselves and have a distorted view of their own importance in the world. Communicating with them effectively is a challenge because they don't listen, unless, of course, you are feeding their egos, which is more about them. They filter what they want to hear, taking what strokes their egos and rejecting anything that doesn't fit into their delusion that the world revolves around them.

- The **Narcissist** cannot tolerate being wrong and brings an unreasonable sense of entitlement to conversations and self-focus to relationships.
- The **Power Monger** is interested in compensating for his or her own feelings of weakness and inferiority by acquiring power through status, people, and things to feel more important.
- The **Control Freak** needs to control not only conversations but people, too, in order to feel good about him- or herself.
- The **Intimidator** wants to establish his or her superiority, often by instilling fear so that others won't speak up.

How to Deal

Don't take the bait. Centers of the Universe will have you as twisted as they are in no time if you play into the game that they are playing with themselves. Stay on track and do not allow yourself to be reduced, because watching you squirm and shrink is how they get their jollies.

What to Say

Nothing. Ignore the bravado, and don't engage in their histrionics—just stick to the facts. However, depending on the situation and your relationship and how secure it is, sometimes it works to push back and say that you don't understand why they aren't listening to what you are saying. If the Center of the Universe is over you, you need to be careful because that ego will fight a bloody battle to win and will not respond well to having its sense of power challenged.

Egoist/Egoista 3: The Buzz Kills

These guys and gals are *negative, negative, negative!* They refuse to explore alternative possibilities or open their minds. They obstruct important dialogue from occurring because they are stuck in a world of small-mindedness.

- The **Naysayer** says that everything won't work and is not interested in anything new and/or improved.
- The **Know-It-All** always has to be right and thinks he or she knows how things will turn out regardless of whether it's true or not.
- The **Curmudgeon** is ill-tempered, full of resentment, and stubborn.
- The **Ignoramus** is not open to suggestions from others and is not open, period.

How to Deal

Ask a lot of questions. Every time a Buzz Kill tries to put the kibosh on something, probe like crazy as to what makes him or her so closed-minded and why he or she feels the need to choose failure over success before things even get started. This retrains them like Pavlov's dog, but instead of learning to salivate, you teach them to think and reason before opening their mouths. At least in your company it will work because your questions become the stimuli that force them to think about how defeatist and irrational their mind-sets are.

What to Say

"Why, oh why must you put such a damper on everything?" With this group, you have to "go there" and keep going until you ferret out the source of their negativity. Make them answer why they are so committed to ruining the spirit of optimism. Then point out how their pessimism is grounded in nothing substantive or real and that whether they know it or not, they're making everything harder than it has to be, including trying to have a conversation with them. If they must be miserable, then ask them to keep their negative ways away from you.

Egoist/Egoista 4: The Slippery, Sly Ones

Watch out for this group. They are underground operators—covert, like snakes slithering through tall grass. They undermine healthy dialogue and erode trust by feigning authenticity and operating under false pretense.

- The **Dissembler** conceals the facts and his or her true intentions.
- The **Skulk** is evasive and shirks responsibility.
- The **Conniver** schemes, lies, and cheats to get ahead, all the while pretending to be on the same side you're on.

- The **Manipulator** bends the truth, twists words, and hides his or her motives as a means to serve his or her own end.

How to Deal

Call them out on it. You have to, because when the ego knows you *see* it, it has nowhere to go and nowhere to hide. Once it's brought to consciousness, normal human beings are typically hard-pressed to continue acting like Neanderthals because they know deep down as well as everyone else that, behaviorally speaking, they are being really, *really* ugly. By merely revealing your awareness of its presence, you will often shame that part of the Slippery Sly Ones into minding their manners.

What to Say

"Something doesn't add up here." Alternatively, you could say, "This does not feel kosher . . . or cool . . . or copacetic . . . or *right*." In other words, guilt the ego into behaving like a human being by letting it know that you know something is off. It is also perfectly acceptable to ask for the real truth as opposed to the fake truth wrapped in a bunch of BS.

Egoist/Egoista 5: The Suck-Ups

We've all known our fair share of these folks. It's their insincerity that makes them so difficult to converse with. They'll "yes" you to death in lieu of having a meaningful conversation and leave you with nothing more than empty words, not knowing whether they reflect the truth or not.

- The **Blowhard** is stuck on him- or herself and full of useless self-serving jabber.
- The **Sycophant** attempts to curry favor by flattering people.
- The **Brownnoser** is motivated by approval and goes out of his/her way to impress those he or she deems "important."

How to Deal

Make it clear that you would prefer not to have a conversation that consists only of agreement and accord. But if that's what the Suck-Up is determined to give you, don't beg him or her to join the conversation. Let them walk away, for it is they who lose in the big picture because their needs will never get met if they are committed to the superficiality of their approach. Hopefully, they will eventually figure that out. In the meantime, it's not worth your time and effort fighting to involve a Suck-Up in a meaningful conversation in which he or she has no intention of participating.

What to Say

"Please stop. . . ." Point out that they don't need to blow whichever way the wind does and that it is infringing on your ability to get anywhere in the conversation. You can also point out that you find them to be very challenging to talk with due to their lack of engagement. Then let it go, move on, and see what happens. He or she may come around—or not.

Egoist/Egoista 6: The Oblivious

This bunch is really "out there." They exist in their own reality, which is unrecognizable to almost everyone else. The problem is that real issues don't get addressed while they frustrate the lucidity necessary for constructive conversations.

- The **Dreamer** is not only *not* in reality but is in denial most of the time, too.
- The **Flake** has trouble connecting what he or she says with what he or she does, and as a result, conversations with this person seem as though they never happened.
- The **Drama Queen** blows everything out of proportion and creates drama for attention.

How to Deal

Have the conversation and cross your fingers that the Oblivious "gets it" because chances are slim that he or she will suddenly enter the real world at that moment. Give it your best shot and document everything that is said. Trust me, when it comes up again, the Oblivious will have no idea what you're talking about.

What to Say

"Snap out of it." You can ask them to try to step out of their own reality and face the facts as they are, but don't hold your breath and don't kill yourself trying to persuade them to exist on this planet with the rest of us.

Egoist/Egoista 7: The Juveniles

These kids trapped in adult bodies get high grades for their puerile ability but are more draining and taxing than a twenty-six-mile marathon. They sap energy, waste time, and turn the workplace into a day-care center.

- The **Blamer** never accepts responsibility for even the smallest, stupidest things and finds reasons to blame someone else.
- The **Whiner** complains all the time about how everything but he or she is the problem.
- The **Excuser** makes excuses for everything and is automatically defensive.
- The **Spoiled Brat** has fits or pouts when things don't go his or her way.
- The **Gossip** stirs up trouble and wastes time being concerned with other people's business.

How to Deal

Point out to them specifically what is juvenile about their behavior. Express your astonishment at the time warp they've trapped you in and see their stunted growth for what it is. This observation goes a long way in managing the turbulence that they bring to conversations. And many times it even puts an end to it.

What to Say

"Please grow up." Sometimes it's best to tell them point-blank how unbecoming their behavior is.

> **When all else fails . . .**
> If the situation is not conducive to you making a statement and you need a less direct way to "out the ego," just turn the statement into a question. For example, "Where is the defensiveness coming from?" "Why are you so angry?" "Are you feeling OK?" It doesn't even matter what the answer is. The purpose is to bring the ego forward to consciousness so that it is unable to surreptitiously undermine the conversation from the background.

You may have noticed that throughout the Ego Patrol, a common thread prevails. All in all, egos collectively share one ugly, universal trait: they exist to serve themselves. Like infants, they are incapable of seeing beyond their own needs, empathizing with others, or creating space for people to be who they are and feel what they feel. In other words, it's all about them. Granted, it makes perfect sense for a baby but simply does not work for adults by the time they are out in the world and earning a living. It's the workplace, not a bassinet. We have to get along with one another, which primarily happens through our ability to communicate effectively, or not. But when you think about organizations and the multitude of interdependencies that rest on the relationships between people, it's easy to see via this lens why and how communications at work present such palpable challenges. You cannot have a healthy and humane conversation without compassion, and if one party is focused on nothing more than him- or herself, a conversation that involves feelings (which all difficult conversations do) is doomed before it even gets started.

The best thing you can do for yourself is to not expect the other person to care about anyone's feelings but his or her own. That includes yours. It's simply out of his or her reach to do so. Until these so-called adults decide to expand their own personal capacity as human beings, it's simply too much to ask of them to engage in heartfelt and meaningful conversations as long as their egos dominate. So save yourself the disappointment and frustration from what others may or may not do and focus on your own communication skills and ability to manage the process effectively in its own right.

That notwithstanding, it is important to remember that the aforementioned *types* do not represent or classify personalities per se but rather the ego coming to the fore and changing its face based on different circumstances. Particularly during difficult conversations where certain situations are likely to hit a nerve, and therefore trigger the ego to appear, you can expect that ego to take a beeline to childhood and bring one of these delightful little characters out of hiding to join the conversation. Yes, indeed, they make it dreadful. What *you* can do is learn to communicate around them. And the easiest way to do that is to remember that at its core, all the drama created by ego is nothing more than insecurity in people who let their egos drive. It's that simple. It's that straightforward. All these people are, and I mean *all* they are, is insecure. It's one word that answers the sum total of all dysfunction in work life and beyond. Imagine the stress, pain, and frustration they cause for so stupid a reason. It's such a waste. Most important, however, it's not your problem. It's theirs.

But why can't it be more easily fixed? It's mind-boggling, actually. We want security, and we want it everywhere. As a nation, we're focused on national security. We schlep to work every day for financial security. Once we get there we work hard to prove ourselves, hoping for job security. We have lifestyles we want to secure, and we look for that in our relationships. We secure our buildings, our computers, our accounts, and our valuables. But we never seem to notice that the security people feel inside is typically the least secure thing of all. Instead, we install more alarms, add to our nest eggs, and write new laws to protect our assets, our futures, and our loved ones when what we really need to do is exert as much energy and focus securing our internal environments as we do our external world.

One way to begin solving the problem is to try and create as secure a situation as you can by learning to balance your ego with that of the other person. The idea is that when you start turning fear into confidence, you can begin moving through conversations with as little pain and as much humanity as possible. At no time can your goal be to interfere with someone's individual growth and/or relationship with him- or herself by wanting him or her to change to suit you. Instead, it can only be to control the effect that that other person's ego has on you while you work on your own weak spots wherever they may be holding you back. Let me repeat. *You cannot fix someone else's ego.* It's too deep-seated.

You can only manage its effect and keep the negative impact to a minimum while you work on fixing your own.

Beware of Power Trips

The other important consideration in handling egos in workplace conversations pertains to the hierarchies that surround us in our business world. Keep in mind with all egos, whether they made our list or not, you need to be careful about which communication strategy you choose to employ. The role of power that is inherent to organizational structures will invariably alter the dynamics and subsequent feasibility of what you can and cannot say. It's unfortunate but true. Power is a sour reality that we have no choice but to accept as members of this great American dysfunctional workforce of ours. But imagine the additional complications when you take into account that those who yearn for power the most often attain it in their attempt to quell an insatiable ego within. So the biggest and most troubled egos often end up "above" those who do not need to prove something to themselves and the rest of the world. In the cases where power is a factor, either implicitly or explicitly, and an unhealthy or fragile ego is "over" you, tread cautiously because it does not take lightly to being bruised and will use whatever power it has to protect its tenuous facade. In other words, you may pay dearly if you go too far.

Incidentally, none of this is meant to imply that egos and the people they're in are unable to create great success. They are. In fact, very much so. I do a lot of ego bashing and draw a great deal of attention to its shortcomings, deficiencies, faults, and harmful effects. Yet in no way am I saying that people who let their egos lead them around by their noses are unable to rise through the ranks, get away with murder, have a winning effect on people, and generate impressive results. That's what makes them so darn slippery, and so Jekyll and Hyde–ish. Egos are charming, witty, charismatic, alluring, and seductive *too*. All good things, most of the time. But like I said, ego breaks the links between minds, hearts, and words. The problem then, when it comes to communicating head-to-head, eye-to-eye, face-to-face, heart-to-heart, and person-to-person, is that egos can't do it because they can't feel for others. They only feel for themselves. So while these high-ego, low-feeling people may very well have a myriad of achievements to point to in their lives, their external development of skills unfortunately occurs at the expense of basic human development internally. As a result, what they lack is the most important thing when it comes to successful human interaction—and that is the ability to empathize.

Finally, to be sure that we cover all bases, there will be times when difficult conversations cause reactions that are equally as uncomfortable as those put forth by people's egos but that are much less combative and defensive in nature. There will be times, for instance, when people in tough conversations just need to cry. Or sometimes they are shocked into silence. But no matter, the same rules apply. Back off and give the person space. It's OK. Just breathe. The difference here is that you don't need to throw up any kind of strategy to protect yourself. You just need to let the person have the experience. Either way, with or without the presence of ego, at its core, the principles are the same. It's about letting people be, understanding what they are going through, and creating enough distance between yourself and them to remain safe and unaffected by whatever means they need to use to process their emotions. The best you can do is act humanely on one hand and contain the destructive impact of the ego on the other. When all is said and done, I can appreciate that egos end up in adulthood to serve what seems a vital function. If childhood ego weren't situated in its rightful place, then there would be no mechanism later in life to invalidate the words that were piped into our heads and left to filter their way through each phase of development that said we were stupid, ugly, selfish, bad, wrong, evil, inferior, invisible, unwanted, not good enough, unloved, or whatever. So like any good little ego would do, it starts producing evidence as soon as it can to prove that none of the accusations are true, and in turn attempts to reverse the pain inflicted by those earliest wounds. See ego run. And then watch its owner try to keep up. It's exhausting. But if chasing things, people, titles, status, and success to disprove something that was never true in the first place it means missing the human experience as a result, I have to wonder how successful, *successful* then really is. I mean, what's the point?

Application

Just for fun, think about the coworkers in your past and present and see how many fit into the Ego Patrol. And, perhaps not quite as much fun, give some thought to whether you have fallen into any of the categories—or ego traps—during some of your own past difficult conversations.

4

Professional Maturity

Everyone has a choice in life. Denial is always one option. Consciousness is another. Yet, there are an awful lot of people out there who seem unaware of the difference and are stuck somewhere between the two as a result. This, however, means trouble for an organization and the information that needs to flow between people. It's also, by the way, torture for all of the *other* people who are not mentally, psychologically, or emotionally hog-tied to themselves by their egos. For every one person who has a healthy understanding of him- or herself and an ego intact, there is another (or two or three . . . or fifty) who opt to ignore the discrepancies among what they say, how they act, and what they do. Let's face it, the split-personality Jekyll and Hydes at work are no fun to deal with. No fun at all. But that's what it *is* to work with people who have been splintered and therefore contorted by their egos.

Now it's all well and good to take notice of what makes people tick, but work is not a shrink's office, nor should it be—*ever*. People don't go to work to be analyzed, and employers don't pay their employees to sort out childhood traumas *on the clock*. Aside from being a deeply personal and private endeavor, working out the relationship that one has with oneself is something way beyond the scope of what's appropriate for the pursuit of workplace goals and initiatives. The two simply do not belong together, although I'll admit that sometimes I fantasize about the integration of a new corporate policy that would be as ubiquitous as FMLA or sexual harassment. In it, I imagine that companies treat dysfunctional behavior the same way they regard other non-work-related indulgences like personal phone calls and shopping on the Internet or tell employees that they have to "do it on their own time." But even if we had such rules in place, they wouldn't work because some way, somehow, those early chinks in our armor come with us to work whether we like it or not. In fact, that's probably how the whole "leave your personal problems at home" mentality started. Meanwhile, what we should have been saying all along is, "Leave your pain-in-the-ass ego at home."

Becoming One at Work

It is the flip side to this stringent separation of personal issues and professional behavior, though, that explains why nothing ever seems to change. Workplace patterns persist, dysfunction abounds, and communications continue to falter *because* we adhere to a model of work that further severs people from themselves. But it's in all the wrong places. We allow egos to come to work and thrive while we disallow people from being human. If individuals in a workplace are unable to see themselves as a whole and the things around them clearly, then it follows that the same disconnection from reality will be true for their organizations. And since this lack of clarity never gets addressed in a substantive way, people become frustrated with work, and companies ultimately reach a state of limbo that is impossible to fundamentally fix. In other words, people are stuck. Conversations are stuck. Communication is stuck. And so organizations, too, are then stuck. It's the ultimate workplace dilemma that has the power to hold organizations back more than anything else.

Admittedly, fixing the entire workforce, raising consciousness worldwide and ridding businesses everywhere of the nefarious egos that plague work results is a bit ambitious. I'll give you that, so let's leave it to the side as our stretch goal. In the meantime, to at least equip ourselves with a solution for getting through difficult conversations, there is an alternative to *either* consciousness *or* denial. And that is to fake it. Yes, pretend to have the maturity of an emotionally developed adult at least during the window of time that you have to endure a tough conversation. That is if you want to survive it, be good at it, and no longer have it riddle you with fear. With that I promise you, in real time, professional maturity, even if it is fleeting, is the key.

Whether it's in you or *the other guy*, on some level we know that there are people who are being ruled by a child inside that governs the behavior exhibited on the outside. We see it, we feel it, and we witness it somewhere in someone every day. It's *that* child who taints the workforce and our efforts to communicate with his or her selfish, infantile behavior, which usually turns out to be nothing more than a masturbatory waste of time. So fudge it when you have to and leave the baby at home, back at your desk, in the bathroom, or on the ceiling for all anyone is going to care. Just do not bring it into the room where you have to face someone and go head-to-head with an honest, unaffected, and uncontaminated conversation.

Like many behavioral things in life such as love begets love and hate begets hate, acting like an adult begets acting like an adult. In most corporate cultures, it's called role modeling. And it works. Not only can professional maturity be contagious, it can also build a better environment and more successful communications all around. Bottom line, a workplace should not feel like a day-care center or high school despite the fact that it often does. So the good news is that you can still succeed if you pretend "as if" you're grown up professionally even if you don't want to or can't attain that same level of maturity personally. If not for yourself, then do it for the good of your coworkers, the good of the organization, and the greater good.

See, the thing is that kids can't do the three most important things that render a difficult conversation easy, which are to feel genuine compassion, understand what it means to be humane, and cut through the mumbo jumbo and be direct. They can't do any of that because they don't know what any of it is—yet. Fair enough. That's life. Well it's *that* part of life. But think about the implications for everyone wearing grown-up clothes (and there are many) who are walking around looking like adults but really possessing the communication skills of little children. It's a bit scary. A bit twilight zone, actually.

You've Gotta Have a Heart

I'll admit that deep down I would love to fix the world and make it a kinder and gentler place with less hate and more love. Lofty goal, I know. I also know that I can't do it. "People don't change." We hear it all the time. And to some extent it is true. But people do grow, which often results in change, if they allow themselves to see the past without dwelling on it, accept the present and what's good about it, and lay seeds for a future that will make them happy. What doesn't grow, what refuses to grow, what will *not* change, is an ego. I'm not going to lie. It also takes courage to experience life free of the baggage that has come to define us or that binds us to the destructive phantom of our egos. The irony is that even though the ego creates intense discomfort, people often choose to stick with it because in an odd and twisted way, it is their proverbial comfort zone, as painful as that may be.

Since the effect of an ego-gone-awry is a brain on overdrive and a heart on lockdown, and the connection between them has long been severed, these two human processing centers have to learn to communicate together before they can effectively do so with others. The heart must catch up to the brain. We can go around and around searching for the secret, answer, silver bullet, magic pill, or panacea. There's no DVD. There's no *Finding Your Heart for Dummies* book.

There's no quick, easy out. In good old-fashioned terms, it takes a conscious effort and willingness to learn. That's it.

Emotional Intelligence

The field of Emotional Intelligence (EQ) did a very good job at taking the study of emotional aptitude mainstream, starting with Daniel Goleman's book bearing the same name. But it lost its traction in real life because the whole idea was turned into academic models, tables, instruments, and profiles. All that did was take us out of our hearts where we feel and put us back in our heads to *think* about how we feel. Remember, egos thrive in the mind. So again, we miss the mark. Here I, too, could follow suit and go on and on burying the concept in more words, frameworks, and theories, but all that does is continue to move the learning out of the heart and put it back in the head. Maybe it's a necessary evil to fill the pages of a book, but in doing so, we make all of this way harder than it needs to be. Fundamentally EQ talks about processing, understanding, assessing, evaluating, and lots of other cognitive functions. Again, a very good start. But all you really have to do is learn to feel what you feel and tolerate it. You don't need to be happy about it. I'm not even saying you have to fully accept it. It's good enough, because in general, egos won't allow even that. They're too closed. So if you can get yourself *there*, you've made a necessary jump toward functioning at a higher level and communicating with less stress and more ease.

Typically when you have emotionally intelligent people in the workplace (when you are fortunate enough to come across them), you also have employees who are professionally mature and quite adept at communicating "the good, the bad, and the ugly" in an effective and humane way. What they are able to do so well is articulate how they feel and discuss it without actually processing those feelings in the company of another professional. They do that privately. It's clean, it's crisp, and all of the right boundaries are in place. To be cultivated both emotionally and professionally means to have followed along the continuum of "human being-ism" that started with a child who thinks only of "self" and learned to take and ends with an adult who thinks of others and has learned to give. That transition from child to adult, from being takers to givers, has everything to do not only with how we cope with what life hands us but also with how we navigate the barriers that potentially get in our way in how we communicate with others.

Removing Roadblocks

There's no shortage of guides and tutorials out there to help people learn to better communicate. However, it's one thing to pursue all of the how-tos and to-dos in search for answers, but it's another to do it in blind consideration of the obstacles that render them useless. Just look around. We are inundated with "five ways to do *this*" and "ten tips to master *that*." But learning, changing, and growing are just not that easy, nor are they accessible in "Three Easy Steps!" This oversimplification has not served us well at all. It's the balance of adding skills while removing roadblocks that creates the kind of synergy that propels progress and generates success.

Take a runner. He can be talented, trained, and practiced. Heck, he could even be the best in the world. But if you throw up a wall in front of him, he is not going anywhere, no matter how much money has been spent, time invested, and sweat exhausted. He will fundamentally be unable to move forward the minute he makes contact with that wall, which, for our purposes here, is the ego getting in the way of talking during difficult conversations.

Said another way, you could consider a dancer. Perhaps she worked tirelessly to be good enough to compete among those in the top echelon. In fact, she could be more skilled, rehearsed, and gifted than anyone else around, but if you threw a bucket of thumbtacks onto the stage, all of her hard work would be for naught. The point is, even if someone becomes truly expert at something and has risen through the ranks as a result, obstacles don't just disappear when ignored, despite many diehard "denialists" who try. Real, viable hurdles that are not imagined, like that of an errant ego, if not now, will eventually get in the way. And all of those people who made their way to the top, even with all of their impressive accomplishments, will have trouble communicating effectively if they discount the obstructions coming from within.

From the Trenches

Speaking of the folks at the top, I have two memorable examples, which occurred with two separate bosses on two separate occasions; both will stay indelibly etched in my mind forever. These bosses were each different in almost every way. One was a man, and one was a woman. One worked in fashion, and one worked in finance. One was married with kids, and one was single and "on the town." One was gregarious and loud, and one was docile and furtive. One was a wild out-of-control bullying brat, while the other was mischievous and disruptive, sort of like Dennis the Menace. But each was my boss, and I came to find out they were both hiding a pesky little ego-bound creature under their respective seersucker and Chanel suits.

Here's what happened. Let's start with *her*. I was part of a sales force managing a territory of stores as an account rep similar to, but not exactly the same as, the example I gave in the first chapter. This was the job I had right before that one. My boss had been normal and quite likable for the longest time. I'd received rave reviews and never had any reason to suspect that she was anything other than what she appeared to be, which by the way was fantastic. She took me under her wing and taught me everything she knew—with great pride, I might add. I considered myself fortunate.

So one day I (as a vendor) was calling on a store in Scarsdale, New York. They sold our products. I was sitting in a meeting with the store manager who was responsible for the flow of merchandise from us to them and from them to their customers. She also oversaw the merchandising of our goods and managed the staff who sold them. Suddenly, a woman from a different part of the store came running into a narrow closet that doubled as a stockroom and tripled as an office. She was frantic, saying, "Where's Donna Flagg? I need Donna Flagg right away! There is an urgent call for her out at the fragrance counter!" She narrowed her eyes toward me. "Are you her?" she asked. Startled, I thought someone in my family had died. "Yes," I said as I sprang to my feet and followed her hurriedly to the phone.

"Hello?" I said.

"Donna. It's *Mallory*," she blurted out. Her voice shook with urgency and demand.

"What's the matter?"

"I need you at a company meeting at 4:30."

"OK. When?"

"Today."

"Where?"

"In my office."

I looked at my watch. It was 4:10 and I was at least one hour away door-to-door, *without* a speck of traffic. Was she crazy?

"But I'll never make it."

"This is not a multiple choice exercise, Donna."

"But Mallory, I can't drive that fast. Plus I need to stop and get gas." That was probably a detail I could have left out. She flipped.

"It's your J-O-B to have gas in that car at all times."

"What? Since when? But . . ."

"When I tell you that you need to be somewhere, I'm not doing it for my health. I'll say it one more time. You need to be there. I don't want to hear any bullshit. Figure it out."

Figure it out? I was speechless. This person on the other end of the phone, I did not recognize. On top of that, she was really, really smart. Basic math of time, distance, and velocity or however that goes, should have been enough to quiet her mania. But it didn't.

I don't know why—naiveté, I guess—but I thought I might reason with her and find a compromise. So I proposed,

"Why don't we start the meeting later? I still may be a few minutes late depending on the traffic, but at least I could make part of it."

Her voice dropped. "Donna, I will not negotiate this with you. You're not hearing me. Not attending is not an option."

I had to ask, even though I knew it stood a good chance of inflaming her more. "So why did you wait until now to call me? All I needed was enough notice to get there. It wouldn't have been a problem had I known."

"You want to blame me now? That's it. If I don't see you sitting across from me at 4:30, I'm writing you up for insubordination."

"Mallory, then you are going to have to write me up because I can't be there. I don't know what to tell you other than it is physically impossible. I don't know why you can't see that or why you scheduled this meeting in the first place. You knew where I was. You get my calendar a month in advance."

She slammed down the phone. Feeling flustered, I packed up my things, got in the car, stopped for gas, and called my dad. Relying on his sound mind and rational perspective, I asked, "Is she nuts or is it me?" He suggested that I begin to evaluate how much my job was worth to me. "There is no reason to start letting someone treat you like this now," he said. "It's a bad pattern and too early in your career." His words hit me hard and he was right. Why would I let someone whom I didn't even really know dish out that kind of abuse? I was lucky. I got good advice. And with that, in the car on my way back from Scarsdale, I started planning my conversation with Mallory and plotting out the words I'd use to resign. But the pièce de résistance was the message on my answering machine that was waiting for me when I got home. It went something like this:

In a wicked pinched scream she ranted, through clenched teeth, "Donna, Mallory. I am seething with you right now. I *cannot* believe that you ignored what I said. *I am your boss,* goddamn it. How dare you go directly against my orders like this? You knowingly defied me, and I will not tolerate it. You were given a chance. . . ."

I hit delete. I couldn't take it.

A Monster Revealed

The anger, the hostility—I could feel it crawl under my skin. I had entered her alternate reality and knew I needed to get out in order to preserve my own sanity and sense of clarity. So that monster? That twisted psycho? It was her ego. I don't know if she woke up that morning and let it out of its cage and it simply went hunting for someone to attack and found me. Or if she was feeling especially insecure that day and my inability to respond to her the way she wanted me to triggered the little demon. Either way, it was clear that a whole separate entity was living underneath her charming, funny lovable self. Whew! What a lesson I learned.

I didn't do anything at first, nor did she write me up or fire me—or say anything, for that matter, which was good because I needed some time to think. Really, what I wanted most was to understand what had happened to her. To have someone transform like that right before my eyes was among one of the most fascinating—and frightening—things that had happened to me in my career. I wanted to learn more and figured that there had to be a field of study that could put me close to some sort of reasonable explanation. And no, I didn't apply for a degree in clinical psychology with a concentration in schizophrenia as one might suppose would be the most logical choice, although I did decide to go to graduate school to study organizational behavior. That was because the work element, not the private details of her life, was interesting to me. Again, it was none of my business, nor did I care how she behaved at home. What I cared about was the effect she'd had on the organization and people she touched. I believe now as I did then that work is not personal. Rather it's a place that gives us an opportunity to learn, grow, be challenged, and get paid in the process. That's not to say that we don't forge deep and meaningful friendships and relationships that ultimately extend beyond the workplace. We do. And that's a good thing. What it *does* mean, though, is that one workmate should not suffer the wrath of another due to the latter's personal issues or lack of internal development. I can't think of anything more offensive than someone spreading his or her garbage and grief to someone else who just happens to be wrongly positioned in an organization. Work forces us into relationships that most of the time we don't choose. But that should not affect the inherent responsibility to keep one's problems from infecting someone else, nor should it be a license for individuals with power to act like cavemen.

Look at Paul Gauguin, the postimpressionist artist. He was a miserable SOB, but at least he had the good sense to spare others from his canker by shipping himself off to Tahiti. So in a nutshell, I go back to my professional maturity concept. If you aren't in fact grown up emotionally and can't pretend that you are when you have to be, then find a job where you don't have to interact with people. Everyone will be better off.

So anyway, the next step was to tell Mallory that I was leaving. This was a conversation that I was not looking forward to, especially now that I'd seen (well, heard) her evil twin firsthand. I was terrified that she might show up and snap again. There had still been no follow-up to the Scarsdale incident, which also struck me as odd. To be that mad? To go to work one day and suddenly need to take out your aggression on a human by turning her into a verbal punching bag? Then to say nothing? I mean, who does that? And why? Well, suffice it to say, I was hoping to find out when my classes started in the fall.

Happily, my actual resignation was uneventful, which at first surprised me. But then it all made sense. Mallory was the poster child for someone who did not develop emotionally and was hiding behind a winning ego. All she said was, "OK." I tried to initiate a conversation about the dynamics between us, how to make it a positive and smooth transition, and expressed my hopes to preserve the relationship. But she wouldn't have it. At first she was silent, like a little manipulative girl who pouts to punish, and then she got back in the driver's seat and curtly gave me a list of everything she wanted done before I left. Charming.

The second scenario was much less dramatic and not abusive but equally as strange. This was another boss of mine who came along years later in my career. He was also very, very smart. Despite that, though, he had this habit where he liked to use coded passwords that could double as pornographic blurbs. So for example, one of the passwords he liked to use was "Miso." But what it *really* meant was "Me so horny." He thought it was hilarious. We also had "Jack Mehoff," a potential candidate-for-hire that my boss amusingly liked to say might be joining the team. You get the picture. He was utterly titillated by his secret language that he shared with what he thought was a group of his "boys," as if it provided passage to a tree house clubhouse. Stupidly, he wasn't aware or sensitive enough to realize that some of the boys were actually men who thought the whole thing was really bizarre for someone his age and in his position. Before long, as news spread, we pretty much all agreed that we reported to a weirdo. We weren't on a grammar school playground, mind you. We were at a major, major firm. But this went on anyway. Creepy, right?

The point here is that both of these individuals looked and acted normal enough enough of the time to navigate their way into high-profile, high-paying, high-level jobs. And at the same time, they are perfect examples of how ego got in the way of their development and prevented them from whetting their communication skills. Eventually, though, in both cases they were found out. But it took a very long time for the truth to prevail. She was a crazy, nutty nut job, and he was a bit of a pervert. And for as long as those egos remained in the way of their growth and human development, they were challenged to get through any kind of normal conversation, let alone a difficult one.

Now in all fairness and credit to the wonderful, fun, and uplifting bosses I've had, I do not mean to say that work has to be filled with a bunch of people acting "old," in order to be an environment that is conducive to effective communications. In fact, on the contrary, healthy egos are bright and youthful. They know how to include others, share information, and bring out the best in people. They also are not threatened by the talents and abilities of others, experience true joy when people other than themselves succeed, are interested in differences, and thrive in diverse environments. But above all, they are open and secure with themselves whereas unhealthy egos are not.

So remember! Wherever there is drama, there is a child in the room.

5

Shooting Straight from the Mouth

Even though I've said it already, it's worth repeating. Reading independent of practicing will not do you any good if you plan to improve your communication skills. Granted, it will most assuredly put more information in your head, which is fine. Just don't expect to see any actual progress in your ability to move the needle, as it were, in the quality of your interaction with people at work. However, with a little effort put toward the application of your cognitive knowledge, you can make great strides. The way I see it, jumping into a difficult conversation is kind of like diving into the ocean. You have to start swimming once you hit the water, so you do. Maybe you don't do it with the grace and skill of a Michael Phelps or Mark Spitz, but you swim nonetheless because you have to. So the purpose of this chapter is to provide you with opportunities to take the plunge into the sea of your own thoughts and feelings and find the words that best communicate what you would like to say.

Reviewing Your Relationship to Dread

A good place to start is to familiarize yourself with *what* you dread and *why*. This will help you not only to develop into a better communicator but also to understand others, by virtue of further understanding yourself. And while the answers to the "what" and "why" questions invariably will have something to do with what you learned to fear, they shouldn't mean that you and your coworkers are crippled in challenging workplace conversations because of it.

I'm not saying that you can unlearn a feeling such as fear. That's a misconception. So we are not going to waste time trying to undo something that cannot be erased. Feelings happen whether we like them or not, and they don't go away. In fact, emotional memory is the same as muscle memory and mental memory. On all levels, we retain our experiences and live with their effects. But that doesn't mean we should be held back and nonfunctional as a result. Bodies and minds are retrained all the time. We lose bad habits and learn to do things differently, which usually means *better*. There is no reason why the same can't be done with emotions. It's simply a matter of learning to incorporate them into our lives differently, sans the fear. In fact, it's the same idea as going to the gym intending to build a certain muscle, rehabilitate an injury, or strengthen a weak area. You need new exercises and a little determination. That's all.

Directions

Take a minute and think about your own most dreaded conversations of the past. What were you afraid of? Why?

Pick one of these conversations and reflect on what was good and what was bad. What made it work? What went wrong? How did you feel at the end?

- **What you said.** Write an outline detailing the main points that were conveyed during this dreaded workplace conversation.
- **How you did.** Check yourself against the five dos and five don'ts below and rate yourself on a scale from 1 to 10, 10 being "very well" for the dos and "very much" for the don'ts.

DO		DON'T	
How well did you . . .	Rate Yourself	How much did you. . .	Rate Yourself
Get over it (*"it"* meaning your own issues), so you could get it over with?		Belabor the point?	
Bite the bullet and get to the point?		Make excuses?	
Lay your cards on the table truthfully?		Fill space and time with empty words?	
Allow any humanistic feelings you had to come through?		Use diversion tactics or assign blame?	
Own what you had to say?		Rush the conversation?	

Total your dos and divide by 5. Total your don'ts and divide by 5. High scores on dos and low scores on don'ts is the goal. Low scores on dos and/or high scores on don'ts mean you have some work to do improving your dos and reducing your don'ts.

- **Given another chance, what would you do differently?** Do you feel that you conveyed what needed to be conveyed? What was missing, if anything? What would you have changed? Did you have the right balance of facts and feelings?

Coming out of Unconsciousness

Let me just start this exercise off by saying that it is not going to be pleasant. Consciousness as a general state of being entails a trip down a painful path, particularly if you are carrying around wounds that you have ignored and left lying dormant to fester for years. But on the flip side, if you're not conscious, you're really not awake in the way you need to be to connect with others, understand their needs, and navigate your way through a difficult conversation. So it's really quite a catch-22—you're damned if you do and you're damned if you don't. But because this book is about attaining substantive and sustainable results in workplace communications, we're going to go for consciousness. This merely means developing enough self-awareness to see beyond your own needs so that you can effectively attend to, and manage, the dynamics that arise during the conversations that you dread with others.

So if you want to learn about yourself en route to learning how to handle difficult conversations better, I warn you again, the initial process may not be all that fun. But neither is recovering from a broken leg. Yet you know that if you want to walk again you eventually need to come out of the cast, start moving, and work through the pain.

The good news is that nothing beats the way it feels to stop repeating the same old patterns and finally being able to function at your fullest potential because you became free from your own self-imposed limitations. On the other hand, if you don't want to know yourself in the process of preparing to stare down the barrel of a tough conversation without fear, you should probably put the book down now and, oh, I don't know, go shopping or have a drink.

Directions

1. List the things you are most insecure about in *both* yourself and your life in the column labeled "Insecurity Today."
2. List the reasons why you feel that insecurity in the left-hand column marked "Source/Origin" along with who/what is/was responsible for making you feel that way.
3. Draw a line connecting your existing insecurities to the person, place, or thing that triggered them.
4. List everything you want in your future in the column on the right labeled "Future/Goals."
5. Draw a line connecting your insecurities to whatever aspiration(s) they are apt to hinder and will most likely block.
6. Look at what you wrote and contemplate the links and relationships between columns. See your insecurities and visualize your fututre goals. Process how each

Source/Origin	Insecurity Today	Future/Goals
Where it all began…	Your biggest obstacles	What you want from life…

Going backward/Looking at the past   Going forward/Looking toward the future

makes you feel. Then isolate your past to your child-
hood/adolescence in your own mind and move on.

7. Separate the insecurities of your past from your
   present-day existence in the workplace.
8. Ask yourself the $64,000 question: Aside from
   leaving the past behind, what specifically can I do to
   render my insecurities neutral and remove them as
   barriers to my growth?

Choosing Heart and Head Words

On a micro level, all conversations, difficult or not, boil down
to the words you use and how you use them. So the question
becomes, how do you select the right words when you have
an infinite number from which to choose? Well, a couple of
things must happen. First, you need to search your mind and
heart and pick the words that best reflect what has to be said
from both a cognitive level and an emotional level. Then
you need to separate them into head words and heart words.
They don't mix well in difficult professional conversations
so it's important that you organize them independent of one
another. Now, the only thing to keep in mind with respect
to head words is that what you *think* and what you *know* are
two different things that both originate in the brain but that
need to be distinguished from one another. This is particularly necessary in cases where the conversation is sticky, awkward, and uncomfortable enough to elicit the truest sense
of dread. Avoid the need to share what you think. It doesn't
matter. What matters is what you know, for it is the single

biggest factor in bringing clarity to the situation. Just make sure you've got your facts right before "going in" because the success or failure of the outcome could very easily hinge on your accuracy. Keep in mind, though, that knowing does not have to be quantifiable in order to be factual. It just means that you have to be sure that what you're saying is true.

As far as the heart words are concerned when the emotional component comes into play, the most important thing to remember is that less is more. It's a delicate balance because without the show of any feelings you will be viewed as cold and inhuman and with too much you will be thought of as hysterical and unstable. I like the 80/20 rule or even 90/10 when it comes to keeping the mushiness to a minimum during professional, difficult conversations at work. Sometimes even, there is no place or purpose to insert emotions at all. It really depends on how long, complex, and serious the topic of the conversation is.

As an aside, while this book is strictly about learning how to overcome, deal with, and discuss challenging work situations, it's worth noting that if you're home or handling matters in your personal life it's another story entirely. In fact, your strategy should be the opposite of what works in the workplace. In difficult personal conversations you'll want to increase what you think and feel and limit the number of facts you throw in the faces of friends, neighbors, and loved ones. The idea for communicating successfully both professionally and personally is the same in that a human connection will make the difference—for the better. It's just a matter of the tone, the tenor, and how much of yourself you share that will vary in order to accommodate what's appropriate in each setting.

Meanwhile, everyone has a verbal repertoire containing words that feel right. Maybe you like the sound, maybe you like the meaning. Or maybe you just like how they convey what you want to say. But even though all words are well, words and for all intents and purposes created equal, they do color a conversation depending on whether they originate in the heart or in the head.

Let's take a few examples from the people I mentioned in the first two chapters and identify what words could come from the head (what you know) and those that might be said from the heart (what you feel).

Example	Head	Heart
The man who wanted his coworkers to get their food out of the refrigerator	Food is rotting. It smells. Needs to be thrown out.	NA. (It's too benign a topic.)
The woman who wanted to tell her boss to stop yelling at her during meetings	Yelling in front of other people. Demotivating.	I feel upset by it.
The man who had to approach his employee about questionable charges on an expense report	Expense not approved. Receipt raises legitimate questions.	I'm sorry. My intention is not to embarrass you.
The woman who wanted her colleague to avert his glance away from her breasts	Not appropriate. Wrong focal point when someone is talking.	It makes me feel uncomfortable.

Directions

Fill in your own head and heart words for the following examples.

Example	Head	Heart
You sit across from a coworker who sneezes without covering his mouth.		
Your boss is playing favorites with a member of your staff, which is disrupting the overall effectiveness of your team.		
A big client has complained that your account representative is emitting a horrible stench and affecting the business relationship.		
A coworker who is also a friend stole your idea and got promoted as a result.		

Now, there is but one thing left to do. Start speaking.

Exercising Your Communication Muscles

By the time careers start, an organic shift should have begun to move away from the parent-child model, where the focus is on what we need and get from others, to a more equalized perspective where as adults, we learn about the mutuality of give and take. However, this only happens authentically and in a sustainable way when the learning is intrinsic and occurs from the inside out.

Talking to Yourself

The first and most important conversation starts here. Read and respond to the following. Don't edit your thoughts, words, or feelings. Speak the truth, including what's good and bad, the positive and the negative.

- *Think.* What do you think about your ability to communicate your thoughts and feelings clearly?
- *Write.* Jot down the words (adjectives) that come to mind and then pick the three best and three worst aspects of your communication ability.
- *Say.* Pretend you are sharing your communication strengths and weaknesses with someone else and practice saying it out loud.

Talking with Others

The transfer of skills happens here. Take a real dreaded conversation from your work life.

- *Find your head.* Start with what you know to be true and/or factual. Write it down.
- *Find your heart.* Add how you felt using descriptive words rather than processing the actual emotions. Write it down.

- *Find your mouth.* Spit it out starting with the words that came from your head and moving to the ones in your heart. Practice by saying the words out loud.

Rewiring Your Hardware, Software, and Emotions

Creating the links from brain to thoughts to heart may feel like a rusty wheel trying to turn at first. But once the connections are made, the relationships between them can begin to forge and eventually flow freely as they are lubricated with practice.

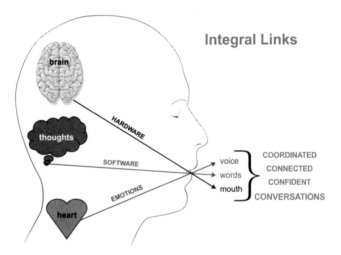

Directions: Free Association

On a piece of paper, throw as many words as you can that pertain to the following hypothetical work situations. Anything that jumps to mind is good. Set a timer for two minutes. Repeat the exercise for each scenario.

- Asking your boss for a raise
- Dreading a confrontation with a coworker
- Apologizing for an error
- Firing a subordinate

Once you have completed brainstorming, look at your words. Take two different colored highlighter pens and for each scenario:

1. Highlight any words that represent factual/cognitive information in one color.
2. Highlight anything that falls into the feeling/emotional category in the other color.

Take a moment to assess how the colors played out. The distribution of your words highlights your tendency to think in more cognitive or emotional terms, which is valuable for you to know going into a difficult conversation. This will help you gauge your balance or lack thereof and show you the lens through which you approach communications.

Understanding Your Communication Energy

If I say it once, I'll say it one hundred times. Personality "typing" is not helping us negotiate differences in communication styles. All this does is box us in and construct more limitations around us. What's more useful in practical terms is to understand the nature of energy that people bring to their conversations. So when it comes to communication "styles," there are really only two factors that you need to worry about, understand, and appreciate. You have *energy* that falls along a continuum of negative to positive, and then there is *intensity* that runs from high to low. Generally speaking, negative energy is not good regardless of how intense or laid-back one is. And with intensity, the biggest challenge is understanding it for what it is and not misinterpreting it as something good or bad. People read intensity wrong all the time and it leads to problems. People with low intensity find high-intensity people intimidating, and high-intensity people find low-intensity people circumlocutious. They turn it into something else like "She's a bitch" or "He doesn't get it," which is not accurate. It's just the intensity with which they communicate.

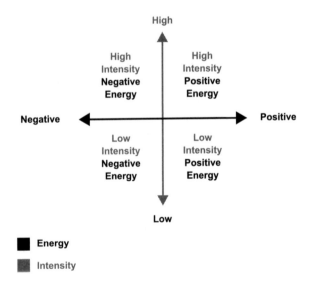

That said, some people need to learn to soften the blow, and others need to sharpen the point. This is where adapting your style by adjusting your intensity and energy can advance your communication skills beyond your expectations. And it beats trying to "adapt" your personality, which—if you've tried—you know really doesn't work.

Personally, whenever I think of intensity, the difference between Listerine and Scope comes to mind. And if you asked people to describe me, many would say, "She's intense." OK, so? I'm Listerine. I am inclined to get to the point and appreciate when other people do the same. The more direct someone is with me and the less peripheral chatter there is to sort through to understand him or her, the better. But not everyone welcomes the zing, the bite, and the sting that can accompany this kind of communication style.

Probably the least likely of whom are the milder Scope folks. They tend to have a less pointed delivery, which at times can also mean they seem less direct. What that means for me and others like me in the Listerine category is that there are plenty of times when we need to temper our intensity with a buffered, more watered-down approach in order to make dissimilar people feel more comfortable. I'm not saying it always works. Remember, it's impossible to control how someone else is going to process and interpret our words and how we say them. *That* in the trade is what we call "baggage," and it belongs solely to the person who is carrying it. But what we *can* do is be aware of how we affect people when we speak and try to be as sensitive to them as possible.

The same goes for the "Scopes" of the world. They may seem evasive or possibly even aloof as compared to their Listerine counterparts, but that doesn't mean that they are nor that they intend to be. It just means that their brains process the flow of information differently and as a result, they deliver it in another way. It's kind of like the difference between a Mac and PC too. Neither is superior or inferior. They're just different—*good* different.

Mark my words, just watch "Listerine" and "Scope" attempt to have a conversation and you'll see why energy and intensity are the qualities that cause either the most harmony or the most dissonance. In other words, Scope frustrates Listerine and Listerine frightens Scope! But once it's brought to light, it need not lurk in the background and impede each one's ability to communicate. So next time you gargle, think about it. Do you bring intensity to your conversations, or do you tend to be more mild in your approach? And from there ask yourself what category others would put you in if you were to give all the people with whom you work a survey.

Distilling Words into Effective Conversations

For many people, the biggest problem in difficult conversations is that they use too many words and become overwhelmed by them as a result. Lots of times it's simply because of nerves and other times it's due to a lack of discipline to self-edit. But by bringing too many words, too many thoughts, and too many feelings into an already complicated set of circumstances, words become entangled into semantic chaos, tongues get twisted, and messages get lost. So the goal here is to learn how to create a quick and easy distillery for yourself so that you have nice, neat conversations with clean edges.

Directions

1. Pick a situation where something needs to be said to someone.
2. Separate how you feel about that situation from what you want to convey.
3. Write down three words that describe both how you feel and the core message of what needs to be conveyed.
4. Lose the three that describe how you feel *about the situation* and keep the three words you chose for what you want to convey.
5. String them together into a sentence and practice saying them as if you were actually talking to that person in real life.

Alternative

1. Put all key words of your message on a piece of paper.
2. Cut or tear out the words.
3. Shuffle, dump, and pull three to five pieces of paper.
4. Connect the words into one sentence.

Finding the Right Diet of Words

Just like you can select foods to eat that constitute a diet that works for you and your body, so, too, can you choose the words that help you say what you want or need to say. But before considering the words themselves, it's helpful to think about how you will organize them. Generally, a little structure goes a long way, and if you set up your flow into a nice, round three-part structure, it will help hold your conversations together. So you need a *setup* or *lead-in* to start off, *softeners* or *hardeners* to take off the edge or add it in once the conversation is under way, and *closers* to finish it off in a cogent and orderly way.

Directions

Go through each of the following scenarios and spend some time thinking about what words come naturally and feel right to you that would facilitate the ease with which you carry out a difficult conversation.

1. Your boss—ask for more money.
   - Set up
   - Soften or sharpen
   - Close
2. Your employee—terminate an underperformer.
   - Set up
   - Soften or sharpen
   - Close
3. Your coworker—tell a peer that his/her alcoholism is showing.
   - Set up
   - Soften or sharpen
   - Close
4. Your client—tell your client you lost all of his or her money.
   - Set up
   - Soften or sharpen
   - Close

Words for Thought: Some Examples

My personal favorites:

Set Up
"We need to clear a few things up."
"There is no easy way to say this. . . ."
"I have bad news."
"Can we chat for a few minutes?"

Soften or Sharpen
"I'm troubled/disturbed/distressed by this. . . ."
"This is not working. . . ."
"I want to talk with you because I care about our relationship and the quality of our interaction." (Sometimes I add, "If I didn't care about you and how this goes, it would be much easier to do nothing.")
"This is not personal. I just have to say what I have to say."

Close
"I'm sorry."
"Thank you."
"What can I do for you?"
"Are you OK?"

Part 2

The Who

6

Employee to Boss

Approaching a superior with anything less than good news can be riddled with stress and apprehension, especially if said superior has taken the power imbued by his or her position to heart. For one thing, at its most banal level, bosses have the power to say, "No." We don't like that. But whether we are requesting something or not, authority in general is not easy to confront. Aside from whatever flashbacks from childhood it may trigger, implicit power over another human being, which can also be explicit at times, is just too weird, restrictive, and stifling in a work environment. It's also too parental, too unequal, and too potentially degrading for the average self-respecting adult. On top of that, we're taught not to challenge authority. So it's no wonder that most people dread confronting their bosses, regardless of the topic. The chances of being met with rejection, embarrassment, and/or disappointment are simply too high to not cause misgivings, reluctance, and, of course, dread. At least in our own minds we make the worst-case scenario true by virtue of anticipating its inevitability. But what seems to be more the case in reality, once we come out of our own minds and into the *actual* conversation, is that it is never as bad as we've conjured it to be in our heads.

I remember having to face the woman to whom I reported in my first job about a drug problem. Or more accurately, it was the effect that her drug problem was having on my coworkers and me, and our ability to go to work and do our jobs. I don't know that I recall dreading the conversations per se, but I do remember perspiring profusely under my clothes and trying to inconspicuously dab the beads of sweat off my upper lip when it came time to ask her if we could sit down and have a chat.

I had issues, two of which were the reasons why I felt I had to have the conversation. First, we had a group of employees who reported to both of us. I was the junior and she, the senior part of a sales management team. She was known to disappear for days on end, dodge phone calls, and leave us wondering whether she was dead or alive.

When she did eventually emerge from who knows where, she reeked of substances that were recognizable half the time. The stench of morning-after alcohol, stale cigarettes, and singed roaches not only were not hard to identify but also offered the first clues as to what she was doing while she was MIA. But it escalated, as most addictions do, and we were left inhaling what we later learned was the scent of crack cocaine. It was not uncommon for her to doze off in meetings or come to work un-showered and wearing the same clothes from the day or days before. And since I was the first line of defense standing between her and our staff, I was caught smack-dab in the middle, left to absorb all of the complaining, bitching, and moaning from the people who worked for us. Meanwhile, there was nothing I could do or say. They weren't wrong. I had no defense for my boss nor did I have the power to do anything about it. I hated being in that position.

Secondly, our business depended on her. I couldn't do my job and make my numbers unless she did hers, nor could anyone else on our team. As a senior buyer, if she didn't issue purchase order numbers for merchandise to come in, there was nothing for anyone to sell. Imagine the Great Depression. Our shelves were literally bare.

As it turned out, I was more eager to relieve the pressure of the vice in which I found myself than I was afraid of her possible retaliation. In fact, it had gotten so bad that I didn't care what the outcome was. All I knew was that I had to say something. I had no choice. So my plan was to tell her that things were not working and that it was because of her. I also knew that the conversation was not going to be about her addiction. It was irrelevant, as nonsensical as that may seem.

Despite the clarity of my thoughts, though, the situation was not without inner conflict for me. What made it hard was that I liked her as a person very much. She was great. Funny. Smart. Warm. But I despised her as a professional. And because of that, I could not imagine how exactly I was going to approach her. Like a friend? Like a hard ass? Like a subordinate? Part of me felt really bad and part of me wanted to rip her apart. Once I came to terms with this love-hate angst, I decided that what I thought and how I felt were the two most honest parts of what I had to say. So I started there.

We had plans to meet one day for lunch. I'd not seen her for weeks. She was four hours late and disheveled almost beyond recognition when she finally did arrive. I was in no mood to dance around the niceties of "How have you been?" and further pretend that everything was fine. So I asked her if we could go somewhere privately to talk. She looked confused but hid it in her lilting voice and broad smile. "Of course we can," she said. "Where shall we go?" I suggested that we go outside and sit on a nearby bench.

Because I couldn't take the awkward disparity of just one of us being sober, I jumped into the words swirling about my head, grabbed a few of them, and blurted out, "Kathy, we have a situation." She looked at me wide-eyed and dewy. Stoned? Maybe. Hung over? Probably. The words poured out of my mouth and funneled through a monologue that followed and went something like this:

"This is really hard for me," I said, "because I like you a lot and don't want this to tarnish our relationship. *But*, I'm having trouble with how things are going. [Heavy sigh.] I'm conflicted actually. It's really hard to manage everything and everyone with you being out so much. We don't have what we need, we don't get responses, we are losing our credibility, and frankly we look really stupid and incompetent. I am taking heat from the staff and the vendors, and it's getting worse. I'm worried about our business and discouraged that irreparable damage is being done to our reputations. But more so, it's frustrating to work so hard and not have the support we need from you. I'll do whatever I can on my end, but it is not going to work unless we come up with some sort of solution now. Otherwise, in all fairness, I'll tell you up front.

If we can't turn this around, we're going to need to get Anne [her boss] involved, because we can't go on like this."

She apologized profusely and said it would never happen again. Apparently, she was going through a difficult personal situation that was coming to a close. She thanked me for bringing it to her attention and assured me that everything would be fine. Well "fine" turned out to be a relative term and nothing changed. Anne did indeed get involved, although unbeknownst to me she had been already. Kathy was fired and I survived, no worse for the wear. In fact, I would venture to say that I was actually better off for it in the end.

What Kathy did for me, which I didn't appreciate until years later, was produce an opportunity that forced me to bite the bullet and blurt out what I needed to say. But more important than that, she took it well and did not lash out, pull rank, or overreact. And with that, my difficult conversation training began. Because she didn't traumatize or silence me, cause shame, or become defensive, I was put on a path of professional and communicative growth that began without fear of retribution. In other words, I was free to keep trying because in my own mind that first experience hadn't gone sour enough to deter my efforts. Each conversation that followed I saw as an important opportunity to practice. And while "success" never meant changing the outcome, as these conversations often don't, I learned that what mattered was the exchange between two people in its own right. That way, "it's" out in the open, and unsaid words are not left to prevent you from moving forward, which is exactly what they often do.

We're All in This Together

In addition to the sum total of my past, which brings with it experiences that I will pepper about as we move through the next few chapters, I have been collecting stories from other people who have also had to face dreaded conversations in the workplace. These various accounts come from friends, family, business associates, and strangers, both online and in person. I've culled the ones that struck me most for any variety of reasons, but all of them offer something for us to look at and learn from. There was one in particular from a man named Tom that I loved so much, I couldn't think of starting off any other way.

Tom's Story

A number of years ago, I was hired as communications adviser to a Canadian cabinet minister in Ottawa. I had my first crisis my first day on the job, and I thought I would probably set a record for the briefest career in the federal government. The cabinet minister's executive assistant (EA) was a bombastic, hard-drinking man who ruled the minister's staff with fear and intimidation. He actually had a sign on his desk that said, "Grab them by the balls and their hearts will follow!"

Anyway, I had hardly had time to check whether the pencil sharpener in my new office worked when another member of the minister's staff burst through the door to tell me we had a problem. The EA (let's call him George) had decided to fire one of the female members of the minister's staff because "she was too fat." While the woman was, in fact, rather overweight, (a) he couldn't legally fire her for that and (b) the consensus around the office was that George had made a pass at her (he was a notorious womanizer when he was drinking—which was most of the time) and was smarting from her subsequent put-down. The staff member who had brought me the bad news told me he had suggested to George that firing the woman was the wrong thing to do—and had been thoroughly chewed out for his efforts. Red-faced and near tears, he suggested that as communications adviser to the minister, it was my job to try to dissuade George because if the incident went public, as it surely would, it would reflect badly on the minister.

Steeling up my courage, I resignedly entered the inner sanctum of George's office. He was puffing angrily on one of the ubiquitous unfiltered Camel cigarettes that would eventually kill him and scowled at me when I asked if I could talk to him. He pointed at the chair across from his desk and said, "Sit down!"

With damn-the-torpedoes-full-steam-ahead resignation, I told George I understood he was going to fire Ms. X. "That's right!" he barked. When I asked him why, he repeated his earlier statement to the other staffer: "Because she's too damned fat!" Knowing such a firing would be in contravention of federal human rights legislation, I replied, "George, you can't do that."

"I can do anything!" George bellowed in reply, fixing me with a stare that said I was a millisecond away from being tossed out of his office and onto the unemployment line.

Figuring I had nothing to lose at this point, I decided to use a line from an old joke: "Can you tap dance?"

George blinked, obviously not expecting that response. He glared at me for a few seconds, then stood up and, to my utter astonishment, started to do a little Bojangles routine.

"Thanks, George," I said. "You've just made me a hundred bucks!"

The man stopped in his tracks, stared at me and said: "What do you mean?"

Borrowing the punch line from that old joke, I replied, "I bet the rest of the staff that within five minutes of being in your office I'd have you tap dancing."

George fixed me with another of his famous scowls and I braced myself for a tirade. Then he started to chuckle. It rumbled deep in his chest and burst forth as a full-blown belly laugh. He reached across the desk, his hand extended. "You and I are going to get along just fine!" he said as he pumped my hand.

George and I went on to have many disagreements, but the young woman in question kept her job and I lived to fight another day!

The Use of Humor

Besides the hilarity of George and Tom and the fact that this one makes me laugh out loud every time I read it, two additional things occur to me with respect to dealing with a difficult boss. One is that if we sized George up against the Ego Patrol, he'd be a classic example of a Ticking Time

Bomb, with his explosive, tyrannical tendencies. The other is the use of humor and how well it works when and with whom you'd least expect it. If you can pull it off, like Tom did, it can be as effectively disarming as any other strategy. I would only say that, like Tom, you need to be prepared that you will be hit with one of two outcomes. Either it will work, or it won't, in which case, you'll be looking for a job. Humor worked for Tom, because it came naturally to him. He rolled the dice and took his chances that being who he really was was the best shot he had. It was a courageous move and it worked brilliantly.

Another good example of a strategy that worked well came from Rich, who was working for a consumer goods company when he hit his boss squarely between the eyes with what he had to say. He illustrates precisely what I mean when I say, "Get it out and get it over with."

Rich's Story

Years ago I was denied a promotion for "political reasons." The CIO of this Consumer Products Company was a true professional; took me out to lunch and told me his hands were tied; the CFO and CEO were demanding the job be given to someone else who wanted/needed to work closer to home for family reasons. He told me I deserved the promotion and the position was rightfully mine. He genuinely felt awful. He promised to "do something" for me.

Fast-forward a bit. The new manager moves into what should have been my position. She sits in her office and cries—yes, cries. She has no clue as to what we do, why we do it, and who we do it for. She is ignoring me and running around to others in the department asking for information, explanations, and help. Because this was the Land of the Cubicles, I could hear every conversation. They all went something along the lines of "Ask Rich. He has that information." Sonia kept ignoring me. The situation was not good—for anyone. I wasn't sleeping; I hated going to work; the department was frustrated; she was running out the door at 4:30 every afternoon, offering no leadership or guidance.

I decided to show her how to be a leader (or get my ass canned). I walked into her office one day, shut the door, and said the following, "Listen, you and I both know I wanted this job. You and I both know this job was mine. But that is not what happened. Now you have choices. You can sit in this room crying and ignoring me, or you can come to grips with the fact that I am here to support you and can make you look very good. I can get you the respect of the rest of the department, which right now you do not have, and you can walk out this door before the rest of us every day knowing things are under control. The choice is yours." I did not wait for a response. The tears were rolling. I got up and walked out.

Things changed—for the better, at least during the next six months, at which point I decided it was time to become an entrepreneur and leave the company.

Granted, that conversation didn't end the way Rich wanted, but the fact of the matter was, by having the dreaded conversation, he forced Sonia's hand and gave her the chance to step up to the plate. Otherwise, he would have dreaded going into work every day of his life at that company.

If only every challenging conversation went as smoothly as Tom's and Rich's had, I suppose there would then be no need for you to read, or me to write, this book. And while it doesn't seem possible before the fact that our dreaded conversations could *ever* be so straightforward and cut-and-dry, you will see as you read through the personal stories that follow, that they are almost never as bad in real life as people make them inside their own minds. This fact in of itself—knowing that we make it worse than it actually is—should help calm the anxiety that accompanies these conversations.

It's Not Personal—It's Business

That said, you want to make sure that you are clear about the difference between the individual and his or her personal problems and the actual situation that you need to discuss. I see it all the time. People constantly confuse the reasons for the situation, which is the part that doesn't concern them, with the impact of the situation, which is the part that does. For example, everyone thought that Kathy's drug problem was the problem. It was so clear, so obvious, and in many minds, so wrong. Well, from a professional communications point of view, it wasn't. I know it sounds weird, but her drug-alcohol problem had nothing to do with what she and I needed to discuss. The only topic we had to talk about was the specific business barriers that her behavior *caused*. Indeed, the addiction and those barriers were inextricably linked for her, but not for me. Bisecting them was the key. So the issue was not why she overslept, but that she was late because of it, or not that she was drunk, but that she missed an important meeting because she was incoherent and forgot about it. So the focus is, and has to be, that the business cannot run under whatever circumstances their problematic behavior creates.

I was lucky—Kathy unknowingly taught me a lot. But Kathy also wasn't a mean spirit. Claudia, on the other hand, tells a story of how she was challenged by a boss who could be as wicked as she was winning.

Claudia's Story

The conversation I need to have that I am struggling with has to do with someone who has a very nasty tongue. In this case, it's my boss, Betty, who is also a friend. She's much older, in her seventies, has been a widow for ten years, and has remained alone. Oddly enough, she works in PR and is incredibly charming to clients and everyone else when it suits her. Yet she has little or no filter between what she thinks when frustrated and what then comes out of her mouth. She'll make the most thoughtless, cruel comments and think nothing of it.

I've encountered this behavior in other people before and always found it frustrating. The difficulty in talking with her about it is that she is so unaware of her behavior. People like Betty are always so surprised at how wounding their words can be. Often they'll just continue to strike out when questioned, so it can feel

futile to call her out on it. Once they're done spew-
ing they feel fine because they've released their "tox-
ins" (and infected other people with their unleashed
anger and frustration). It's very much that of an addict's
behavior. They can be told repeatedly that what they
do is destructive, but they can't and won't stop themselves because they enjoy the release too much.

In the case of Betty, people repeatedly quit working
for her because they couldn't endure her rages. Often
it is over something simple but she'll escalate—a paper
tray in a printer is unfilled and she screams, "Nobody
ever does anything I ask!" Or a phone call isn't returned
and she'll chide, "He never does his job."

But recently, what kept me up at night was that I'd
said something relatively innocuous at which Betty
took offense and told me to "shut up" in front of my
other colleagues. It's like working with an alcoholic,
and I know it'll happen again.

Jeez, another one from the Ego Patrol. Not that it should
come as any huge surprise. They're everywhere. Except this
one is part Ticking Time Bomb and part Oblivious. Here's
the deal:

- Betty "makes the most thoughtless, cruel comments
  and thinks nothing of it," *because she thinks of nothing but
  herself.*
- She "can't and won't stop herself because she enjoys the
  release too much." In other words, *she gets her kicks by
  inflicting pain on others.*

It's ugly. And, unfortunately, I don't think Betty will show much interest in growing up at the age of seventy. But heck, you never know. It's one thing to be twenty-something and not have it all together. That's normal. And it's also the point, I suppose. You can't be nearly as hard on the younger generations because they have not had an opportunity to learn and apply that learning to their professional growth. But the older ones? I'm sorry—as time goes by, expectations should change, and the correlation between, age and civilized behavior should increase with time.

But with people like Betty who tend to be mean, things get thorny (regardless of age) because abuse is a pattern that extends way beyond the reasonable parameters of work. It should not even play into the equation, but unfortunately it does. And regrettably, an abusive person in the workplace is death to a healthy and productive conversation. The most you can do is have a go at it. Go in strong, say it like it is, and be prepared to make a graceful exit in the event that your attempt backfires. Otherwise, sticking around in a place where you sit and fester in that kind of energy will kill you and your spirit. It's certainly worth a try, but if it doesn't work, find somewhere healthier to work for your own good and let those who want to be miserable, be miserable without you.

The other thing that I found interesting about Claudia and Betty was the fact that a friendship existed between them. I would have thought, that as friends, it would have been easier to discuss hurt feelings and that having a personal relationship would have increased the likelihood that Betty would have cared about how Claudia felt. But that's not the case, and so my question is, who needs friends like that? It's bad enough to have to deal with it in a boss. But Betty squared? I'd pass. Thank you very much.

This next one wonderfully illustrates my mantra, "It's not about working it out, it's about getting it out." I like to think of the words that make up these conversations as loose change in your pockets that needs to be emptied. You can't carry it around forever. It gets heavy. So it can be helpful to imagine a similar process when you're trying to "unload" what you have to say. Reach in, dig around, pull it out, and lay it on the table.

At first blush, I suspect that you'll wonder how I could think that Frances's story is a good example of anything. Admittedly Keith, Frances's boss—who by the way is another poster child for the Ticking Time Bombs (maybe we should have a pageant)—leaves a bit to be desired in the area of tact. But that's OK. Why? Because each of them said what he or she needed to say, each person made it clear to the other where he or she stood, and it ended with no ambiguity. It may not have been a lovefest, but at least Frances and Keith could move on and not have the silence of the situation immobilize them.

Frances's Story

Keith, a supervisor for more than a decade, was a very explosive character. Most of the time I ignored his outbursts. But one time, there was an error in my records that, even though it wasn't my fault, was a major error and would have to be reported to upper management. He went ballistic and I went into hysterics. After a few hours, I calmed down and told him that I would have been willing to stay late to fix the problem, but he had upset me so much that I was unable to do so, since he had made me feel ill. His response was that this was his personality, and he wasn't going to modify it. My reply was to ask him, in a very reasonable tone, if he understood that his behavior was counterproductive and that I was not going to accommodate him. He shrugged and said, that was the way things were. So I left him to deal with it himself.

Granted it would have been *so* much better if Keith took Frances's words to heart, looked her in the eyes, and expressed his regrets for acting like such a buffoon. Clearly, as a result, we saw how Frances had no desire to hang around and help him after being treated as she was. And if this were a management book there would be tons to talk about why and how a gruff, dour, and cantankerous manager like Keith is not the cream that rises to the surface, nor is it the way to bring out the best in people. But this *is* the reality of the workforce. He blew it. Not Frances.

Frances had the courage to say what she wanted to say. That was the most important thing for her. Maybe Keith didn't respond the way she would have liked, but that doesn't matter as much. She was smart, methodical, and insightful enough to give herself time to calm down before presenting herself to him as an emotional mess. Again, you can't control the outcome. All you can do is say what you've got to say. And Keith? He did the same. That's why I like him here. Remember, the purpose of these conversations is not necessarily to get what you want or to change another person. Yes, wouldn't it be wonderful if people were clamoring to oblige our every wish every time we brought our woes forward. That's not how the world works, much to my chagrin. But if you approach things with the objective of eliciting information that helps you better understand another person, and the situation, then at least you're clear and armed with what you need to know to make the right move for yourself. I respect Keith for saying, "This is how it is." It was honest and all Frances needed to know. Maybe his intensity and energy didn't suit her, but at least she knew what she was dealing with and was free to respond in whatever way she felt was right for her. This is the volley at work that I think is all too often forgotten. You give me information. I give you information. And we take it from there. It may not feel as safe. But it's honest and it creates a path forward.

And then we always have the situations that don't necessarily go as well as we may have liked. Nina, a writer for a major network, put her boss in his place when he upbraided her publicly. In cases like this, though, it comes down to the cost of saving face, which at moments like this, is worth a lot, but not without a price.

Nina's Story

I was assigned to write for primetime TV for an extremely high-profile show. In a loud voice, the star of that show said, "I've never had a woman writer before," making eye contact with everyone on the set. He had given me a scene to rewrite, and seconds after I handed it to him, he bellowed, "This is crap! This is garbage!

I can't read that." I could feel my face flushing from embarrassment, but I was determined not to leave the set in shame. Taking a deep breath, I smiled at him to make sure we made eye contact. Then I said, "Yes, I know. It's terrible. But don't you think you should read it first?" He turned red, ran into his office, and slammed the door. The producers all came over to congratulate me. About a month later, he apologized. But I never felt comfortable working with him, and he probably felt the same way. People I didn't know came up to me in the halls to say, "Aren't you the one who embarrassed Joe?" and they would shake my hand. It was god-awful.

Nice comeback! But it wasn't free. This is a classic example of what can happen when you take a calculated risk and "purge" your thoughts into words on the spot. Ideally if faced with a similar situation, you want to take a second and compare the short-term gain with the long-term effect. In the end, it's a roll of the dice either way because both our jobs and life in general don't come furnished with a crystal ball.

And yes, while I am a big proponent of "blurting," Nina's story does reinforce that it has the potential to make things worse and not better. So it has to be up to each individual to decide what his or her own tolerance level is and then try to make the best decision from there. Nina didn't face worse-case scenario and get thrown out, but relations were strained and perhaps not the best that they could have been either.

Moving on, Michele's story takes us full circle as she epitomizes how people torture themselves for no good reason. The greatest value here is to ask yourself—*and answer*—why?

Michele's Story

It's over now, but it certainly kept me up at night.

I have been married for ten years and have two boys aged eight and six. I had been working outside the home for all of that time. Partly due to finances, and partly due to the health insurance as one of my children has a heart condition and ongoing medical expenses. My husband had finally gotten to a point in his career (he had gone back to school and changed careers during the course of our marriage) where he was making more money than me, as well as having employer-sponsored health insurance. We had additional personal responsibilities as well, as we live next door to my aging parents. Everything finally came to a head, and we decided that I needed to quit my job in order to focus on our home life.

That's all fine and good, but I needed to tell my boss. I was an executive assistant to a vice president at a major film studio. I had been working for her for four years. I knew that this news would hit her hard, both personally as well as professionally. It took my husband and me three months to make the final decision and decide when to put my notice in. Throughout all that time, I was going to work like nothing was wrong, which made me feel deceptive—a feeling I detest. The day came when I decided to put notice in. Since I had control of my boss's calendar, I determined when to talk to her privately. I had this big whole speech prepared. It was going to be professional, and courteous. While I knew that this was the right thing for my family, knowing I was going to cause all this change for my department was very unsettling to me. I asked to speak with her, shut the door, sat down, and promptly burst into tears. I was mortified! My totally professional plan was completely ruined. I managed, between sobs, to explain what it was that I was doing. She totally understood. Perhaps the tears helped, I don't know. The conversation I dreaded for months was over in ten minutes. And a box of Kleenex.

Now, I know I said earlier that emotions should be held to a minimum in order to properly manage a difficult conversation and ultimately direct it toward a positive outcome. *However*, in Michele's case, which may appear to directly contradict the "little-to-no-emotion" rule, she ended up communicating through her tears, which inadvertently expressed her feelings by supplanting her words. That's OK though because it wasn't her ego crying. It was her. In fact, it was good because underneath all of the strategies, tools, exercises, and scripts offered in this book, what matters more is that you are comfortable bringing the most honest version of yourself to the conversation. That's what Michele did and by doing so, she was human, the conversation was real, and it worked out fine.

Asking for a Raise

Along with resigning, asking for a raise or promotion can be equally as unnerving a task, if not more so. Employees feel paralyzed by the mere thought of posing the question, to the extent that they often end up accepting lower earnings rather than having to face the subject with their boss. So as the topic of more money repeatedly came up during the story-gathering process of writing this book, I noticed that some interesting and recurring themes emerged in response to my question, "Why are you so afraid to ask?"

• **My boss is cheap and will never say yes.** My response: That's your boss's problem, not yours. You can still ask. You never know. Plus, you can't be sure unless you try. And if company frugality is at the expense of fairly compensating employees, you may want to reconsider your desire to work under those conditions in the first place. That assumes, of course, that you are not being paid a competitive salary for the job you have.

• **I shouldn't have to ask. More money should be a reward for the good job that I do.** My response: Yes, in a perfect world that's true. But the world is far from perfect. And beyond that, having such an outlook prevents important performance conversations that enable a shared understanding between a boss and an employee. Without that understanding, a meeting of the minds on compensation will never be achieved. The point being, if you wait for it to happen, chances are good that it never will. Think about it: it would be a rare occasion that a company seeks out opportunities to spend more money on payroll. However, that does not mean that the company wouldn't find the money if presented with the idea and a persuasive argument to support it.

• **I'm afraid that bringing it up will make it weird to interact with my boss in the future if the answer is no.**

Then, I'll think he or she thinks I can't do my job, or am not doing my job. You know, like I'm not really worth it. My response: Whoa. Where to even begin? First of all, a salary is a line item on a budget. Do not let it become entwined with your personal self-worth. They are two different things. And if you are not doing something right, better that you should find out sooner rather than later so that you increase your chances for an increase at some point before *never*. Bottom line is that you need the feedback either way.

In her own words Vicki explains why asking for higher wages feels like such an insurmountable and impossible feat.

Vicki's Story

I'm pretty low on the corporate ladder, and I've always worked for small firms. So when it comes to asking for a raise, there is not a big corporate HR structure to go to. You speak with your direct superior instead. The reason I don't ask is fear. It's the fear of rejection, which is what asking the question could lead to. If "they" don't want to give me a raise, then there is obviously a disconnect between what they think I am worth and what I think my work is worthy of. It also might suggest that I, the employee, am not as happy as I could be or want to be. So asking for a raise could bring this disconnect into focus and in turn result in tension in the workplace.

Perhaps the employer starts thinking, "Hmmm, this employee wants more money. She might try to find a different job that will give her what she wants." This will either encourage the employer to offer the raise in order to keep the employee or start questioning if they really want that employee in the company at all. And when you're low on the ladder, like I am, you often don't have much leverage with which to negotiate.

This pretty much means your ability to grow within the firm will be limited. It also causes you to doubt yourself, which may result in a self-fulfilling prophecy. To avoid this, the company should ultimately proactively offer the employee a raise.

This thought process also kind of extends to negotiating salary when being hired for a new position. If you're not being hired for a top position, you have less leverage with which to negotiate. Having said that, many people change jobs seeking a higher salary, so how do you do that if you're not a VP?

OK, there are a few problems here. Primarily, the thinking is flawed. First of all, talent is talent regardless of level. And a job well done is a job well done regardless of title. Companies need good people irrespective of how high up on the corporate ladder they are. However, the time that position does matter is when you need to determine how your salary measures up against the prevailing rate of pay for a similar job in the marketplace. It's very possible that you are being paid as much as, if not more than, the average person with comparable skills performing parallel functions in other companies. That could make it hard to put forth a convincing argument. Additionally, if that does turn out to be the case, what you really need to be asking for is an opportunity to prove yourself so that you can be moved into a "higher" position, which would then no doubt correspond with more pay. So do a little homework first in order to be unequivocally clear about what you need to ask for. You may find that it's not a raise per se but a path to a promotion instead.

Secondly, it's not a game. Or at least it shouldn't be. To assume that an employer will pay more to avoid losing an employee *or* suddenly start questioning that employee's value to the organization just because a request for more money was made is all screwed up. The fact is that no one knows what someone else is thinking unless that someone else is given a chance to share his or her thoughts. If they don't want to lose you, they don't want to lose you. That will come up in the conversation, not because of the threat that you might leave but because you created the space that was necessary to discuss and explore your contributions to the organization. Having said that, even if you are considered a valuable asset to a company, it's not always possible to change salaries just like that. Don't take it personally. It's business. It's the way it is. But most importantly, it doesn't require so much convoluted supposition that in the end only accomplishes one thing. And that is to paralyze the person who needs to have the conversation.

As an aside, just in case anyone is having similar thoughts about asking for a raise, it's worth calling out that thinking or hoping that an offer outside one company could potentially improve your chances of a salary increase inside another is not the kind of strategy that pays off in the long run. Especially if you are thinking that the suggestion of which will manipulate the very response from your employer that you are afraid to elicit directly by simply asking yourself. It doesn't make any sense. It's just a conversation. Think of it as dialogue. And don't be afraid of your boss. He or she is just a person like you.

Meanwhile, by all means, if an opportunity should arise elsewhere organically, then let it. And if it's a good one, seize it. That's valid. Careers are cumulative and based on the sum of their parts. Every move you make is important because it is strategically linked to what came before and what will come after. One wrong move can throw off your trajectory for years to come. So avoid the risk and save yourself the trouble of a mistaken derailment by just asking if a raise is possible. If the answer is no, *then* you may decide that you want to, or need to look for another job where you can "bump up" your salary.

Just keep in mind, though, a mentality that your employer might want you, or want you more, if someone else does is a dangerous assumption. While it may be true that many a counteroffer exists, it's an unreliable way to go about securing your own income. It's like the equivalent of trying to make a boyfriend or girlfriend jealous in your personal life to get him or her to want you, independent of your own merits. It's a shortcut that robs you of the truth on one hand and the opportunity to overcome your fear, learn to communicate, and develop trust and respect in your relationships on the other.

Finally, my greatest caution of all goes directly to the biggest mistake I see people make. Don't predetermine the outcome and draw conclusions about another person's response when it has been fueled by your personal fear and is not grounded in reality. No one knows what *will* happen. Predicting the future is only an attempt to protect from disappointment, but all it really does is defend against possibilities. It's just your ego again raising hell and telling you that what can happen can't. But egos have nothing to do with "today," nor are they authorities on anything.

So when the time comes, this is what you want to do when asking for a raise:

1. Evaluate how competitive your salary is. In other words, if you were to go to another company with your existing skills and experience what would they offer to pay you? Ask around, go on the Internet, do the research.
2. Give some thought to how happy you are—or not. There are many intangibles in a workplace that add value. Are you learning? Are the people supportive? Do you like your industry? Do you like your job? This will help you weigh all of the factors related to your level of satisfaction in your job and prepare you to have a more comprehensive conversation beyond, "Will you pay me more?"
3. Organize your thoughts. Write down what makes you a good employee. Specifically list what contributions you've made to the company and business. Rehearse it, or do whatever else you need to do to make it clear in your head.
4. Structure your conversation. Set it up with what brings you there. Perhaps you should highlight

the positives. Then, deal with the crux of the conversation, which is your need or desire to make
more money. Make sure you back up your position
by explaining how and why you feel you are being
underpaid (assuming you are). Remember, realisti-
cally speaking, a company can't say yes to all the
people who believe they deserve higher compensation because that would pretty much include everyone. You have to be convincing and persuasive by
laying out the facts of (a) what you are worth in
the marketplace and (b) your intrinsic value to the
company, its health/culture, and its bottom line.
And finally, close the conversation by either asking if an adjustment to your salary is possible now
or in the near future, or if you can discuss a path
with milestones attached that will prepare you for
growth and promotion.

So whether you're asking for a raise or you need to
approach your boss with any other subject you dread, your
greatest position of strength is to be crystal clear about what
the stakes are and how far you are willing to go. This will
help you to not flounder, be clearly understood, and, most
importantly, narrow the power gap. It will also lower your
risk of losing control of the situation or yourself.

All told then, when we extrapolate the themes from these
stories, the following threads reveal themselves from which
we can learn, incorporate, and apply.

- Assess your expectations and ground them in reality.
- Calculate your risks.
- Don't go in thinking you are going to transform another person.
- Don't vest all your hopes in one specific outcome.
- Appreciate when someone tells you the truth even if you don't like it.
- Use an approach and words that come naturally to you.
- Be who you are—*do not* try to be someone else.
- Remember, don't torture yourself. It's most likely not going to be as bad as you think.
- Stumble if you must. You'll learn from it. Next time will be better.
- Do the best you can. No one is taping or grading you. Rather, appreciate the learning.

7

Coworker to Coworker

Talking with peers or other people outside report-ing lines about unpleasant subjects can be every bit as dreadful as having to have a difficult conversation with some-one "above" you. But it's different. In these lateral discussions no one person has the power to punish or penalize the other. As a result, the fear of being squashed by the "upper hand" is typically not the issue, although having the conversation escalate into a fight often is. And why not, right? There are fewer structural and organizational parameters in place out-side the hierarchy to prevent it from happening.

The other thing I have long found perplexing about peer-to-peer communication, and even boss-to-employee at times, is the prevalence with which people dread saying what's true and on their minds because they are afraid that the "other person" won't like them as a result. I don't get that. It's preposterous actually. If you are dealing with the type of person who would not like you *because* you speak the truth, why would you care about what that individual thought of you in the first place? They're not worth it. They can't see. They're too small. And for those who can handle it, they'll respect you for having the courage to address them, one human being to another. Even so, despite the logic, this dynamic occurs in the workplace *all* the time. I watch people agonize over confronting someone because they are convinced that it will bring with it reprisal and alienation. But like I said, if that's the case, so be it.

Certainly though, not every conversation ends in rejection or a fight. In fact, most don't. Yet, the thought of having these conversations still manages to make people feel physically ill and overwhelmed. One such conversation comes to mind told to me by a friend and colleague who works in human resources for an investment bank in New York City.

Marley's Story

Here's how the story went. There was a mystery knife. It was covered in peanut butter and left stuck on the counter every morning, but only after it had been smeared around enough to make everything else gloppy and sticky. It wasn't long before the complaints started funneling into the human resources department. No one could figure out who it was or why it was being left there to make such a mess when there was a sink right next to it, a dishwasher underneath, and napkins and paper towels readily handy.

Weeks went by without a clue, but not a day passed without the appearance of the anonymous peanut butter knife. At first, the staff was curious, perhaps even slightly amused. But with every passing day, frustration mounted and employees began to express disgust.

Surely the culprit had to be the most inconsiderate, most self-absorbed, and rudest person on earth, unaware of his or her surroundings and all the people who co-occupied them. Well, that sentiment mushroomed and HR suddenly felt the need to hold a strategy meeting to prevent a minor fury from turning into a case of major "kitchen rage." They decided a little sleuthing was in order, figuring their best and only option was to enlist the help of one of the trustworthy souls who came in before anyone else and could discover and then reveal the identity of the guilty party.

In just one day, they found out who it was. Of course, to make it all the more nerve-racking, it turned out to be one of the most senior executives at the company. The next thing my friend knew, she was being nominated to approach him on behalf of the company, share its collective concern, and ask him to stop. She was horrified. In her words, "I couldn't believe it. I felt ridiculous and dreaded having to bring such a silly thing to this guy who was one of the top in the firm. But I had no choice. So I did it. I caught him in a quiet place in the hallway and I just did it."

"Benjamin?"

"Yes, Marley."

"Can I talk to you for a minute?"

"By all means."

"OK, first of all, can I just say that I am horrified that I have to even say this to you . . . ?"

"OK. What's up?"

"Do you by any chance have a habit of using a knife in the morning with peanut butter on it?"

"Why, yes I do."

"Well, apparently, it is left on the counter, making quite a mess and upsetting a few people."

He smiled. She took a deep breath in.

"That's so funny," he continued. "But, actually, there is some logic behind it."

"OK."

"When I arrive in the morning, it's early and the dishwasher has not been emptied yet from the day before. To avoid putting a dirty knife in with the clean dishes, I hang the dirty knife slightly off the edge of the counter right over the dishwasher. This way, when the cleaning crew comes in, they will know that it's waiting to go in with the day's dirty dishes."

Marley smiled. "I should have known there was a good reason."

A good reason is right! Talk about a well thought-out plan! Not only that, but it was also based in good intentions. Besides it being comical that this little knife caused such a ruckus, it shows how badly, and quickly, things can turn emotional and be blown completely out of proportion as a result. Meanwhile a whole group of people was ready to crucify this guy. Marley, on the other hand, remained calm and simply asked the question. But most importantly, she structured the conversation well by saying what was on her mind and telling Benjamin how she felt before she got into the bit about the knife. Then she raised the issue with the knife succinctly and gave it context with a brief explanation, but not too much. And finally, the conversation ended on a high note when she said that she knew there had to be a reasonable explanation, which there was.

The Art of a Question

After talking with Marley for a while about this and other conversations that she has dreaded in her career, I realized that she had a pattern and a technique, of which she was unaware. Like in the example just given, I learned that Marley likes to start out with a question. When I asked her why that was, she told me that it made her feel more comfortable because it helped her ease into a dialogue without feeling as though she was attacking or accusing someone of something. So by allowing room to create that understanding first, she establishes a "setup/lead-in" that works for her. That, by the way, makes this a very good example of what I mean when I say that it's important to spend some time figuring out what comes to you most naturally. For some people, an opening question could have the opposite effect. Depending on one's intensity and energy levels, the very question that Marley might ask to warm up a conversation could be the same question that one finds aggressive and offensive coming from someone else.

It's not unlike the ubiquitous eye contact argument that has penetrated the world of work decorum, where we're told to look someone in the eye at all costs. Well, on the wrong person, eye contact is outright spooky for the same reasons—it's not natural. If you don't manage your innate gaze, glance, or stare, to work with who you are and how you think then you heighten your risk dramatically of coming across as weird and possibly off-putting—no doubt the opposite effect of what you're looking for.

Anyway, I like questions, too. But for me, it's always the same one, "Can you do me a favor?" It works like a charm to set up or lead into mostly anything you want someone to stop doing, like peeing on the toilet seat, sneezing on your key-board or monitor, unloading his or her work on you, leaving personal trash in the conference room, keeping smelly sneakers in the coat closet—I could keep going. The list is long, but you get the idea. It's simple. "Could you do me a favor?" Pause. "Could you please take your sneakers home tonight?"

Now, usually HR gets the dirty work when it comes to saying the things that no one else wants to say. Lots of times it's for legal reasons, but it's also because there is an assumption in organizations that that's what HR is there for. I don't agree with that but will say that being an HR professional doesn't mean that the words of a difficult conversation automatically roll off the tip of the tongue.

Grace was working in the HR department of a financial-services firm when she found herself in the middle of an awkward situation with two of her coworkers. She struggled with what to do about their behavior, which happened to break the very rules their department was expected to set, exemplify, and enforce.

Grace's Story

Our human resources group of three consisted of Jack, Jill, and myself. We all worked well together and had a good relationship with our manager, Mark. I felt really fortunate to have such pleasant coworkers, a fair boss, and a healthy and harmonious team.

Things slowly started to change, however. More and more often Jack and Jill would disappear. I began to notice a pattern—that one would leave and a short time later the other would also go somewhere. They would both be gone for a while and then one would return followed a few minutes later by the other. It dawned on me that their working relationship had evolved into something more. I didn't want to interfere with anyone's love life, but I had two dilemmas facing me. Number one, I couldn't do the job of all three of us and number two, we were in human resources.

The company policy was explicit. Employees could not date other employees within the same department. And any other employee who suspected, or knew of, such a relationship to exist was obligated to disclose it to human resources. Imagine! What was I to do? How could I look the other way when I knew our policy was being violated by the very individuals who were in charge of enforcing it? If I said something to Mark, would Jack and Jill know it came from me? Would that be the end of my comfortable work environment? And what if I was wrong? How stupid would I feel? But then again, how could I not say something as a human resources representative fully aware of the policy and my responsibilities to the firm?

I was never the gossiping or tattletale type, so this was really pushing me against my nature. Why couldn't I pretend that I didn't notice and just leave things as they were? I seesawed back and forth until I finally realized that our group couldn't function like this and I would have to say my piece. I finally walked into Mark's office and without any pretense just said how uncomfortable I was having to say this but I was doing my duty so I would just say what I needed to and told him that it appeared to me as though Jack and Jill were more than coworkers and it might be in everyone's interest to transfer one of them out of the group. To my relief, he had the same hunch that I had and he thanked me for speaking up. He said he'd handle it and he did. Jack transferred to another group happily and was able to openly continue his relationship with Jill.

One of the things that this story highlighted for me was how easy it is to forget that there is bound to be a reasonable solution on the other end of the conversations that we dread. I think sometimes we get so caught up worrying about the conversation that we lose sight of the fact that it is merely a bridge that connects two points. It's functional, not emotional. For Grace, those two points were the suspicion of an inappropriate affair and protecting the business and her department. For Marley, it was the presence of a knife covered in peanut butter and quelling a group of people who were becoming increasingly upset by it.

Processing Time

Another observation and perhaps even more valuable is how Grace managed her own personal process. She had to figure out how she felt and then from there what she was going to do. She gave her thoughts an opportunity to settle, and, like Marley, she expressed how she felt about having to raise the issue to begin with, which paved the way for a sensible and healthy conversation.

Furthermore, by adding the suggestion to move either Jack or Jill out of the department, she grounded the conversation not only in company policy, but also in what was right for the business rather than in the salacious details of an office romance. Again, it's worth noting here that the conversation is not about the reason that a person(s) does what he or she decided to do. Rather, it's about the connection between that reason and the impact it has on the company, employees, workflow, results, and organization's reputation.

Even though this conversation technically took place between Grace and her boss, the core issue was really between her and her coworkers. Alternatively, Grace could have also gone to Jack and/or Jill directly with the same honesty, approach, and even words. It would have been fine—for her. They, on the other hand, would have had to decide their next move and figure out how to best handle their relationship as it related to their positions and the policy.

Next, we have someone like Maggie, an executive assistant pushed to the point of needing to have a conversation with a coworker who was taking advantage of her. Ultimately, it boiled down to her devising a way to use the conversation to be clear with someone on one hand and break a pattern of behavior for herself on the other.

Maggie's Story

My name is Maggie. I love my job. I am one of the top executive assistants to one of the top guys in one of the top law firms in Los Angeles. My boss is a sweetheart, as they say in the business—a gentleman and a leader.

He is highly respected as well as respectful of me. But *man*, do we work!

Because I am a senior assistant, I've become the go-to person in our department. "Ask Maggie this; ask Maggie that; ask Maggie, ask Maggie, ask Maggie." I hear it all day long. That's nice. My ego loves the attention, most of the time.

See, what happens in firms like mine is that assistants function in work pools where they cover each other to ensure that the attorneys are never left without support—not for one second. So, when new assistants join the team, I meet with them and show them the ropes, so to speak. Then, before I know it, they are asking me to train them, help them, show them what do to. It starts out fine. "Can you help me? Can you teach me? You are great! Oh my gosh, thanks! Can you show me? Can you tell me? May I ask you a question? If it weren't for you . . ." Blah, blah, blah. Blinded by the compliments that continue flowing, I keep telling myself, "It's not a problem," as they end up becoming more work than my own job. Well, what I've learned is that it's not a problem, until it's a problem.

So recently, Karen, a new assistant, came in and was assigned to the desk next to me. She was very nice, educated, and appeared to be well put together. We started training. She thanked me every hour, every day. Meanwhile, in reality, she had no regard for me whatsoever. She'd stroll in hours late, leaving me to bear the burden of her duties *and* mine. Phones rang that needed to be answered, lawyers came looking for her when they needed something done, and their important documents fell behind schedule. That left me covering for her, picking up the slack, and unable to effectively do my job.

At first I was concerned that Karen had a serious health problem. But after the fourth or fifth no-show, combined with her cockamamie excuses for being out, my mild suspicion turned to wild fury. Plus when she was there, all she did was goof around and care not one bit about the burden she'd become. In fact, whether she was there or not, both her absence and her presence were a distraction. I started falling behind and missing little things. I could feel my edge and sharpness slipping away. I was losing focus at my own desk, in my own job, because of another person's shenanigans. I knew it was crazy. So, one day I decided that I had to "let it go" before it got more of a hold on me. So I went into the office with a new resolution. I was seizing the day. I would take the day as mine and focus on my work, on my desk and stay in synch with my boss. No chitchat, no joking around, no wondering whether she'd come in late, leave early, or show up at all. No, just a day of plowing through all of the work that had accumulated around me. And I did it. I was an animal on a mission. It was a great feeling. There I was in the middle of a super day. Flying. I loved it. I was back in my groove.

As timing would have it, though, it was just a little later that afternoon that a colleague came by my desk to say, "Hi." She also said something that made me laugh. Meanwhile, Karen, sitting next to me (essentially pouting all day from not getting any attention from me), said, "Weelll! That's the first smile you've cracked all day." The comment was dripping with sarcasm and so undeserved. I was pissed. The entire office heard it, and they were as astonished as I by the comment. I responded, "I'm working!" After that, I held myself steady and calm. And I waited. I know by now in life, when I am feeling like this, it is best to keep my mouth shut, knowing that the comment that was made was reflective of the person making it versus the person receiving it. After cooling down for several hours, I asked Karen to join me in a conference room to speak. I had to get it off my chest. We both sat down and this is what I said:

"Karen, I know you and I have become friendly in the past weeks, and it's obvious that we get along. You are a very nice person—young, talented, and I adore you. I need to tell you what is going on with me, though. Due to all the chatter, your need for my attention and lack of consideration that I have a job to do, too, I am feeling off my game and starting to miss things. I can't afford that. I can't lose control of my own job, because I'm assisting you to get control of yours. My requests for quiet space have gone unheeded and you have been disrespectful of my time and my schedule, so I have made a decision to focus on my work, and put my attention on what my boss needs, versus everyone else here. That includes you. I still like you as a person. Please do not take this personally. I wish you well. You and your boss are on your own two feet now, so let's leave it at that. And I'll go back to focusing on my boss and me.

"One last thing. That crack you made on the floor was completely uncalled for, and it surprised me. I would like that kind of behavior to not happen again." She responded, "Oh, I didn't mean to hurt you." I said, "Fine, let's let it go, and let's get back to work. Good luck, you'll be fine." We stepped out of the office, she to what was hers, and me to what was mine.

Meanwhile nothing really changed. While Karen may have been clear about where I stood, her nonsense continued over the weeks that followed nonetheless. She basically continued to do whatever she wanted. So when she didn't show up for work yet again, I was bothered by it and struggled with how to manage my own anger and frustration. It was clear that another conversation would be useless. Then it came to me.

It flew into my brain like a shot. *YOU'RE FIRED!*

It landed on my shoulder like a touch. *YOU'RE FIRED!*

It beat in my head like a pulse. *YOU'RE FIRED!*

I said it to myself. I said it to my heart. Then suddenly, all of the negative energy moved away from me. It was glorious, clean, and cool—like a blade. It calmed me down and separated me from all her drama. To detach from an unhealthy person like Karen in a professional relationship was so freeing. I'd always thought it was something that applied more to personal relationships. But those two simple words did it. I separated from her and her manipulative and solicitous behavior. They also helped me stay out of her path and no longer have any expectations at all, quite frankly, for her to even walk in the door. To me, she's not here. It was in my head and my heart and down to my toes. *You're fired. You're done.*

Do I like this person? Sure. She's very nice, is lots of fun, and would be great to chat with at a party. But, when it comes to working with her and getting sucked into her games at work? No thank you.

OK, so there is a lot going on here. First of all, while we have the chance, let's call a spade a spade. Karen belongs on the Ego Patrol. She's a mess, a Slippery Sly One, completely self-absorbed and unable to see anyone else but herself. Nice, huh? So Maggie did the best she could to reach her, but unfortunately it didn't work. That happens a lot with egos in action. I told you, they're pesky little creatures. Once they bite down, they don't want to let go. So because it's no one else's job to pry them off but the rightful owner to whom they've attached themselves, all you can do is say what you've got to say, cross your fingers, and hope for the best. But most of all, you have to make sure you are free of their effect, so you can function and succeed in your own right. That's what Maggie did when she "fired" Karen in her mind.

What I liked about Maggie's approach was that she spoke from both her head *and* her heart. It was proportionately balanced well. Not too much warm-and-fuzzy stuff, but enough to ground the conversation in honesty and frame it within the context of a discussion occurring between two human beings.

The other critical aspects of this conversation were in how Maggie stayed calm, held steady, and had the presence of mind to wait before launching. That came from her self-awareness. She knew enough about her triggers to know her reaction needed to be well timed. But she also had the clarity and maturity to know that Karen's flippancy had to do with Karen and not her. Plus, what also helped keep the conversation on track was that it was all business. Maggie made the focus about work exclusively and was sure to communicate what Karen could expect from her from that point forward. All good.

Conversely, though, Maggie's is also a classic example of when a conversation doesn't work or doesn't change someone. So with that, it's important to note how Maggie went on to what I like to call Plan Be. She didn't spin her wheels trying to get Karen to see the light. She made space for both Karen and herself to "be" who and what they are. Indeed, as was true in this scenario, it sometimes means making pretend that the toxic person doesn't exist. Translation? Workplace survival!

This next story, from Emily, draws into focus the difference between the conversations that *should* happen versus those that *must* happen.

Emily's Story

I teach at a college in Boston and am one of about twenty-five instructors who all teach the same class. I have been teaching there for two years and am a junior/part-time faculty member. There is another instructor who has taught across departments, for years. When I was out of town, he subbed for one of my classes.

I found out when I returned that not only had he not taught my curriculum (very clearly mapped out with times delineated, copies made, and clear instructions written out for all), but he had shown the class a video about the history of the computer (filmed in the '80s) and let the class go early (resulting in that one class, of my three sections, being a week behind upon my return). Then, when asking me to cover for two of his classes (as was our agreement), he did not give me any curriculum but said, "Just teach Chapter X, students can take notes if they want to, don't sweat it, and if you end early, let them go." The second class I subbed for was the final exam, and he didn't provide the exam. He gave it to a student helper, who was twenty minutes late. The exam was open book, and questions were limited to true/false and not particularly challenging when considered against the standards set forth by the department. I was truly shocked by the lack of rigor, preparation, and respect for student-centered learning.

I'm really stuck on how to proceed. I brought up a few curriculum issues (lack of), and he brushed them off, saying, "If students want to learn, they'll get the info." Well, I believe *we*, as the teachers, are there to facilitate their learning by actively creating environments for success. If I go to the department, I feel like a mole. If I go to him, pearls before swine?

This is a tough one because while it appears as though Emily *needs* to have the conversation, I'm not convinced that she *has* to. With the conversations that we think are necessary, but that do not fall into the "do-or-die" category, there is a risk that you will alienate the person (been there, done that lots of times). So you have to ask yourself if it's worth it. In the end, the slacker's job is his own responsibility and it's up to the organization to figure that out and deal with him directly. I doubt that Emily's job description has anything on it saying that she is expected to report on how others who are not subordinates function in their respective roles.

Now, having said that, let's assume that Emily shares the course and co-instructs it with this man and that she is subject to a compensation plan that is based on adhering to the school's standards and meeting the course's requirements. Then she would *need* to say something, because under these terms, she is responsible to the organization for the job she'd been hired to do—and share. And the conversation with the co-instructor could go something like this:

> **Emily:** I am troubled by something and need to talk with you about it. I do not feel as though we are complementing each other in the course and, therefore, don't feel we are providing the best quality that we can. I'm concerned that we are not fulfilling our responsibility to our students.
> **Slacker:** If students want to learn, they'll get the info.
> **Emily:** I don't agree with that approach. They pay for an education and it is our job to provide it. That's what we're here for. Unless . . . Do you not want to teach?

From here the probe should continue in an attempt to ferret out why Emily's teaching partner is so disengaged. Chances are quite good that by exploring his lack of conscientiousness, something important will be illuminated that they can then address together. From there they can map out a plan that takes both points of view into consideration and makes them both happy—or not. The slacker may decide it's time for him to move on to another job where he cares more about his level of input and quality of output.

What lessons can be learned from this chapter?

1. No matter what you think is going to happen or why someone does what he or she does, you're probably wrong.
2. Consider if a conversation is absolutely necessary.
3. Provide yourself with an opportunity to think rationally and logically and work through your own process.
4. Pursue a solution but don't delude yourself into thinking that the solution translates into changing someone or getting your way.
5. Don't waste your time imagining all the things that can or will go wrong, because they probably won't.

8

Boss to Employee

There's no doubt that managers get the lion's share of difficult conversations in the workplace. They are the ones who face the most pressure to communicate uncomfortable messages and/or deliver bad news for no other reason than it comes with the job. Personally, I know the feeling. I've had a few doozies myself. Along with the experiences that have reinforced what I've learned I *should* do during difficult conversations, there was one episode in particular that taught me what *not* to do—not ever, ever again.

At the time, I was a young and fairly inexperienced manager who blew up at an employee. Initially, I was so angry that I was afraid to open my mouth. In fact, it felt as though my jaw had been wired shut. Unfortunately, though, it hadn't been enough to stop me from lambasting a woman on my staff who had taken it upon herself to pry, probe, and perpetuate half-truths that turned into full-blown lies about me. Apparently, she'd become overly interested in my personal life and felt compelled to research the people close to me, gather information, and draw conclusions that ultimately made their way through my department in the form of fanciful tales and sometimes malignant rumors. So right or not, when I found out, I let her have it.

It's not that she wasn't totally out of line and deserving of a disciplinary conversation. She was. But by the same token, I did not need to lose my temper in order to get my message across either. In fact, I would argue now that had I forgone the emotional reprimand, I'd have been far more effective. The only thing I really accomplished was to embarrass someone who worked for me. Looking back now, I would not call it a constructive or productive conversation by any stretch of the imagination, not because of what I said, but because of how I said it.

Showing Restraint

Given the chance to do over, my message would remain exactly the same. Her behavior was totally inappropriate, beyond unprofessional, and moderately malicious. I was right not to tolerate it. I had to say something. She was hurting, not helping our efforts, our department, and ultimately our business. The responsibility was mine to right the course she was on. Otherwise I ran the risk of having her busybody negativity distract, metastasize, and infect the rest of my staff, and in turn the quality of our output. But all I had to say to her was, "No more. Not ever again," without the volume and expletives. And so this is how we learn.

In my case, what had inflamed me so was feeling personally invaded by this person who didn't know me at all. Clearly, she took liberties. She had no right. And it was because she crossed well-understood boundaries that I responded as defensively as I did. But remember, defensiveness comes from ego and will never be the mechanism that enables one to conduct sincere, forthright, and effectual conversations. My story is a case in point.

On the other hand, there are also conversations that happen in the workplace that *are* personal in nature—sometimes so personal that it makes you cringe—and do need to be communicated out of sheer necessity. I happen to think that it's this inherent separation between personal and professional lives that makes these types of conversations especially dreaded. You see, we have this universal understanding, shared and accepted by everyone, that we are personally and professionally divided—that work is one world and home is another and ne'er the two shall meet. But think about the implications of this when it comes to having to speak with someone about his or her personal hygiene or image. Managers are expected to, and indeed do, have extremely personal conversations with people all the time with whom they don't have personal relationships. Heck, managers barely even know each other in any real sense of the word, yet they are left to suddenly pierce this barrier that says "work" relationships should never get that close. So we, as managers, end up being forced to discuss things like body odor, body parts, and bodily functions with employees. Ugh.

Along with having to fire someone, these intimate topics tend to be the worst and most highly ranked on the list of commonly dreaded conversations. So there you are, a sitting duck, telling someone that his or her "scent" is garnering complaints from bosses, teammates, and clients alike.

Melinda Day-Harper, CEO of T-Zone Consulting, shared her story with me about having just such a conversation.

Melinda's Story

I have been managing people for more than twenty-five years. The most awkward conversation I had to have was with an employee who had a problem with body odor, so much so that her coworkers complained to me about it. I really didn't know how to approach her in a way that wouldn't be offensive to her and affect both her work and our relationship. After much thought and a little research, I called her into my office and shut the door.

I began by telling her what a great job she does and how important her contribution was to the team. Then I told her that there is one small problem she may not be aware of that I'd like her to work on. I then said, "I've noticed that you have a body odor that is less than fresh. Now, I've had that same problem myself on occasion, so I'd like to discuss it with you and let you know the things I changed in my routine that may help you."

She was, of course, embarrassed but at the same time eager to fix the problem. We discussed taking showers in the mornings before work instead of in the evenings, washing our clothes after one wearing, and using a body powder that keeps us smelling fresh. During the conversation, I reiterated her contribution to the team.

When all was said and done, she appreciated being informed about the problem from someone she trusted, put in place the things I suggested, and the problem went away.

This kind of awkward, very personal conversation could have gone either way. The important thing to a positive outcome was to praise her work, emphasize her ability to work well with everyone, and gently introduce the subject.

Melinda's story offers some helpful techniques that will be good to know and good to have in your bag of tricks should you find yourself tiptoeing around this embarrassing subject.

- Broaching it as if the person is unaware of the "scent" he or she is emitting is a great approach. It provides adequate space for him or her to act surprised and express interest in resolving the problem.
- Saying that you share the problem is wonderfully humane, whether it's technically true or not. Knowing they're not alone is comforting to people and also helps mitigate the sense of embarrassment.
- Focusing on the job and the work being done softens the blow and makes the odor issue secondary. Sometimes, one of the most effective things I've done has been to preface the "bad" information with, "Look, I think you're great, and I really enjoy working with you." You'd be amazed at how much comfort those few words provide to people and how dramatically they can dissolve what could otherwise be hard-to-manage defensiveness.

- Flat-out saying, "I need you to work on this" or "It's an issue," is what it's all about. It's clear. No mixed messages. No minced words. Straight to the point and not a big deal. On occasion I've also opened with, "This is a sensitive topic and not easy to discuss. But . . ." That has also been received well—or as well as one can expect.

The woman that Melinda spoke to was lucky in the sense that she got the message from another woman. It's one thing for these conversations to be same-sexed, but there are times when the conversation lands in the lap of a man who has to speak to a woman or vice versa. That's what happened to T. David Lee.

T. David Lee's Story

As a long-time supervisor, I've had to tell employees that family members had died unexpectedly, that a fellow employee had been gruesomely murdered by her husband, and that a coworker had run off with a maharishi. All true, but the most uncomfortable one was the discussion with a female subordinate in which I had to explain to her that her coworkers (all female, too, by the way) could not stand her—how should I put this?— pungent odor. Bad enough that I got this assignment at all, since I was the only male in the department, but what made it worse was that I was asked by the woman to describe the smell. . . .

OK, TMI! Let me just stop this right here and make a point. While this conversation was headed toward T. David giving his employee *way* too much information (which he did), I don't think it has to come to that. Rather, I would recommend one of two things happen here. Either recruit a woman to have this conversation, or stop short of describing the gory details. Why? Because odor is subjective and widely open to interpretation. Frankly, it didn't matter what she smelled like, it just mattered that she smelled. From there, it should be up to her to figure it out.

Another blurred line between personal and professional behavior happened when Carol had to talk to her assistant about too much physical touching.

Carol's Story

KC was a lovely assistant. She was cheerful, upbeat, and always willing to help out. There was just one issue: she was too touchy-feely . . . literally. Her maternal instinct led her to take my hands in hers if I mentioned that I was cold or to put her hand to my forehead at the slightest thought I could have a fever. It was too close for my likings, but what could I do about it? I began to avoid speaking around her in case it might lead to an encounter. The office wasn't the place for this type of touchiness for me, and I was getting really uncomfortable, not to mention scared of the next bear hug. How could I say something to my well-meaning assistant? This was just her nature and I suppose it meant she felt some level of closeness to me. Saying something about it could be a slap in the face. I would never want to offend her, but how could I explain that I preferred a hands-off relationship? I agonized over this, wondering if it was better to grin and bear it rather than cause her any discomfort. But I knew that all of the physical contact was making me uncomfortable at the place where I spent most of my life. Finally, I bit the bullet during a casual conversation standing at her cubicle and mentioned in an offhanded way that I was not really the affectionate, touchy type and had noticed that she was just the opposite. With that lead-in I went on to ask her if she could put up with my pet peeve of not wanting to be touched and just try to leave me comfortably in my affectionless state. We both laughed and were then able to joke about it. She became more aware of her actions and the amount of touching was dramatically reduced without ruining our relationship.

What is great about what Carol did here is that she made herself the brunt of the "joke." So it came across more as though she were asking KC to accommodate *her* shortcoming, so as not to make her assistant feel that it was a flaw on her part. KC was a people pleaser to begin with, so naturally she'd be eager to make her boss happy when given the chance. Another important aspect about Carol's approach is that she kept it light. She didn't have a sit-down or feel it necessary to call too much attention to the issue. Just a simple conversational comment in passing did the trick.

Trudy, who was a director of advertising for a large communications company, took another approach when having issues with a woman on her team, but in this example, it was related to the appropriateness of what the woman was wearing.

Trudy's Story

There was one woman in particular who always had some trouble understanding "professional dress." I would chat with friends and other respected sources about how to tell her that most of the time her dress was inappropriate. Her blouse would fall open showing her entire bra. I could almost report the color of her underwear (peekaboo G-string) on a daily basis. I eventually found a way to sit her down and explain to her very nicely that perhaps her coworkers were not taking her seriously because of her attire. Men and women were finding it hard to concentrate when presented with "the girls," who always seemed to be standing at attention. She was mortified and had no idea. From that day on, no dress code issues.

The personal dress issue seems to go one of two ways. Either the individual is mortified, as in Trudy's example, and expresses deep gratitude for the heads-up or he or she takes the feedback as a personal affront—an invasion on his or her personal identity and style. And because of that, I've seen that many people approaching the topic were afraid to because they did not want to offend the other person's sense of self. Admirable indeed. So the thing to do is exactly what Trudy did, and that is to approach it as though you are offering insight to help these individuals understand how they are being perceived and position it as necessary advice that will help them succeed in and advance through the workplace.

Then there are those people who just can't seem to get it together. Due to whatever crazy, quirky habits they have, they remain challenged in the workplace with behaviors that simply cannot coexist within a professional work environment. Jodi tells her tale of having to face an awkward situation with an employee, which started her on the difficult conversation path at the ripe old age of twenty-three.

Jodi's Story

> I was twenty-three and a manager for a major retail store. I was living in Aspen, Colorado, at the time. There was one foreign girl, who, when she was on the sales floor, could be seen scratching her . . . ahem . . . crotch—sometimes with her hand actually down her pants. (This story still makes me cringe.) My head manager asked me to have a conversation with her to let her know that such behavior was not OK. The next time I saw her, I called her into the manager's office and did sit her down for our conversation. I told her that when she was on the sales floor, she needed to be professional and hygienic and that having her hand down her pants for any reason at all was completely unacceptable. I obviously told her that if she did it again I'd have to write her up. It was a horrible conversation to have to have. But I had it nonetheless.

Touché! And these are indeed the exercises that build our muscles. Jodi got an early start. But no matter when the opportunities present themselves, it is often best when you are simply thrown into the situation, because you are then forced to just do it. And over time, "doing it" is what transforms fear and reluctance into skillfulness and confidence. Moreover, like many of the conversations we've visited so far, a basic pattern exists that underlies many difficult conversations. There is what needs to be said—for example, "It's not acceptable" and why. And then there is what will happen next—for example, "You are going to lose your job if it continues." If you can whittle your conversation down to these basic tenets, you'll be off to a good start in any performance problems.

Nicola had a situation that epitomized the need to realign an employee's attitude. She wrote in and asked for advice.

Nicola's Story

What do I do when, as a supervisor, I ask one of my subordinates to come into the conference room and she says no? I can't pull her out of the chair. There are half a dozen subordinates sitting and listening to our exchange with keen interest. I can't have our discussion in front of them. If I walk away, she gets the upper hand in our relationship. Inside, I'm thinking, "Why can't she get hit by a bus?" Outside, I'm trying to be mature, reasonable, yet firm. How do I *make* someone do what I need them to do? In this case, I told her that I would speak with her later in the day. I waited until I saw her leave the room, presumably for a bathroom break, then followed her out. Without an appreciative audience, I again attempted to talk with her. But I deeply resented having to manipulate her into doing what she should have done in the first place.

Totally unacceptable. OK, first of all, it's true you don't *make* someone do what you need him or her to do. You can't. At least not without looking like a jerk in the process. But you can frame the situation for people with important information, present them with the choices before them, and then let them decide. There is a conversation here to be had for sure. And by all means it is one you can have in front of the others. In fact, you should, just in case any of the people in the vicinity were thinking about acting so disrespectfully. This conversation will most likely prevent them from opting for that path in the future.

It may go something like this:

> **Manager:** Suzie Q, could you come into the conference room please?
> **Suzie Q:** No.
> **Walk up to her calmly.**
> **Manager:** I'm sorry, did you say no?
> **Suzie Q:** Yes, I said no.
> **Manager:** OK, well, that's not an acceptable answer here. We don't refuse to cooperate with others. It doesn't exist in the organization. So here are your choices. Join me in the conference room, or join me for a conversation that documents this and potentially commences the termination process. Up to you.

Then stand there and look at her until she decides. If she doesn't move, write her up. Give her one chance, see if it has motivated a change of heart, and if she pulls that stunt again, let her go.

Firing Someone

And speaking of terminations, what would a book on difficult conversations be without a discussion on having to fire someone? No doubt, it's a situation that tends to come with a lot of stress, guilt, and nausea. There is no silver bullet on this one, but there are some things you can do to shift the lens through which you present the information, which in turn can help improve both your confidence and your delivery.

First, understand that employment is no different than any other two-way relationship. And like any other two-way relationship, things don't always work out. Relationships end all the time, not because it's anyone's fault, but simply because there is no chemistry, it's the wrong match, wrong fit, wrong time, and so on. So what I've found to be extremely helpful and effective is to just say those words in some way, shape, or form. For example, "This is not a good place for you." Or, "This environment is not bringing out the best in you." And when it is a performance-related termination, the heart of the conversation is simply, "This is not working out. We need to part company." Some people like *sever*, while others like *separate*. I've heard lots of variations. The point is that you need to find whatever words make you comfortable and use them.

From there the most important point to drive home is that everyone needs a place where he or she can be successful. If a certain job in a certain company does not provide that opportunity to an employee, then why not cut your losses on both sides and make the way for someone to find a better fit where he or she can thrive? Time and time again, I've had people thank me for being honest with them, for pushing them out of their comfort zones, and for caring about what happened to them.

More complicated are the terminations that result from layoffs, though, because presumably then there aren't necessarily any performance issues that have informed the decision to let a group of individuals go. In fact, things may be working out just fine with many of the employees who end up "on the block," which means that it's feasible they are in good standing and have given you no reason to think they belong somewhere else. Much tougher.

The best you can do is go in quickly, remembering how it feels to rip off a bandage versus peeling it off slowly. Get to the point and get it over with—but not without feeling. Where I find the biggest mistakes are made here is that the "terminator" tries to distance him- or herself, which makes this painful situation hurt even more for the person on the receiving end. This is when you need to heighten your sensitivity, be compassionate, listen, show caring, and soothe the employee to whatever extent you are able. There is only so much you can do, but what you don't want to do is come across as cold, hurried, uncaring, removed, uncomfortable, and inhumane. Certainly, you can't change the situation and that has to be clear. It is what it is, and people understand that deep down. But you can walk away feeling proud of the way you handled it and good about your ability to comfort and connect with a human being struggling through an extremely trying experience.

On a lighter note, there are sometimes stories that simply speak for themselves. David was particularly challenged when he tried to explain to one of his employees that she was being downsized. It's a classic.

David's Story

Years back, I had to tell three of my employees that they'd been downsized. (One female thanked me for noticing she'd lost weight!) The word had not been part of the lexicon for too long, but the first two people got the drift very quickly. This young lady, who was selected because of her tenure, not her prodigious waistline, didn't get it at all. I think I told her something like, "We've reached a point where we need to downsize," to which she replied that she was way ahead of me and thanked me for noticing she'd dropped a few pounds. She was so anxious to relate her weight-loss story that I had to sit patiently for about five minutes until there was a break in her monologue. I then made the mistake of trying to cure her misunderstanding by telling her *we* were reducing the size of the staff. This only made it worse, because she then volunteered to help out by putting together a diet and exercise program. Sweet woman, but clueless. I finally got my message across by telling her that it was the *number* of people we were reducing, not the *size* of the people. The aftermath was that the company's fortunes reversed quickly and she returned about nine months later for a rehire interview. Recalling the pride in her weight loss, I congratulated her on her pregnancy, only to be told that she wasn't with child. She'd gained back all the weight she'd lost and put on about thirty additional pounds. She was rehired, but thankfully by another department, sparing me any further discomfort.

And finally we have Jami Bernard, an accomplished writer, film critic, and business owner who was recently faced with a grueling termination. That's not to say that the termination itself was so bad—in fact, quite to the contrary—but it was what Jami did to herself that is most instructive of all. Namely, it's what continues to come up over and over, story after story. *Get it out. Get it over with.* Don't assume you know what someone else is thinking or feeling. And know that if you are grinding and churning inside, it probably has nothing at all to do with the actual conversation, but more to do with something you need to learn about yourself.

Jami's Story

My liberal arts degree and twenty years as a film critic did little to prepare me for running a business. But when I started my own company—Barncat Publishing Inc., where I help writers finish their books—I found that entrepreneurship is largely the art of the spin. Screwing up is referred to delicately as "a learning opportunity." At a start-up, it's one learning opportunity after another.

After nine months in business, there was suddenly a learning opportunity I couldn't seem to face—dropping the axe on my assistant, Lenore.

I knew I had to do it, but I couldn't. I felt bad for her. I had been supporting Lenore and her three-year-old twins for nearly a year—which, in self-help parlance, is "doing something good for your fellow human being" and in reality is "making a mercy hire," something everyone tells you never to do.

I hired Lenore because I wanted this wonderful young single mother to know that someone in the world would extend a helping hand. By the time the adrenaline of my impulsive offer wore off, I realized that Lenore had many fine qualities, almost none of which suited the job I had wrapped around her like a fluffy hotel bathrobe. I spent more time undoing Lenore's damage than she had spent creating it, and it was getting harder to paper over my poor hiring decision with the glass-half-full euphemisms of the self-help industry.

Perhaps it was true, as I had suspected all along: I'm not tough enough. Everyone knows you can't run a business if you're soft.

I was soft. I was squishy. I invented "work" to keep Lenore busy. I hadn't paid myself a salary yet, and Lenore's babies were dimpled and rosy.

I had to let her go, but I couldn't face it—the guilt, the horror of it, and . . . the words! What words could I possibly use? Here I am, a writer and an editor, bereft of any vocabulary with which to perform a simple human-resources task.

I'm not tough enough. I couldn't sleep. I loaded up on salt and fat. I was depressed. Then my depression turned outward—a healthy sign!—and I was angry. I could save Barncat if only I would tell Lenore the truth, that there was no work for her.

In my twenty years as a film critic, I never had a problem voicing my opinion and making it stick. I have been on radio, TV, "Oprah." So why is it that I can't face down someone in the workplace—*when I own the company?*

I suspect it has something to do with my mother.

There was the time I almost did it. Lenore had made a heinous mistake on a simple assignment, leaving me in the position of appearing to break a contract. Instead of lowering the boom, I paused for dramatic effect and, with impeccable enunciation, uttered the F word.

Who's soft? Not me!

By the next day, I was hip-deep in self-flagellation— groveling and apologizing, offering Lenore more work for which she was further unqualified.

It's a pattern.

One weekend, my physical, emotional, and financial distress reached a tipping point. Fever. Sweats. Skin breakouts. Pallor. On Monday, I called Lenore and let her go. I would have burst if I hadn't.

It went something like this:

"Lenore, as you know, Barncat is doing well by the standards of a start-up. But the business has not grown fast enough to support your salary, so I'm afraid I'm going to have to let you go. Take three weeks to finish what you're working on [business code for "time to look for another job"], and of course I'll give you a good recommendation."

I spoke clearly and unhurriedly and immediately felt better, calmer. I didn't collapse into the "It's not you, it's me" protestations I always used when breaking up with guys where it wasn't me, it was them.

I did not turn into a pillar of salt. Neither did Lenore. She said she was "proud" of me for doing the right thing for Barncat.

Dear, sweet Lenore. She of the bright eyes, the occasional brilliant idea, the adorable babies. Someone should help that girl. It just can't be me. My latest learning opportunity has taught me that I can't help anyone if I don't put business first.

In between "tough" and "soft" is the calm, straight, clear, and lucid truth. You don't have to choose one or the other. You can be both if your words are honest.

9

Employee to Customer/Client

Like it or not, customers and clients require us to be on our best behavior. We walk on eggshells, bite our tongues, and tiptoe around the things we're afraid to say because the last thing we want to do is upset the company's cash flow. And it is because this dynamic exists that client relationships tend to require a tone of formality and respect, which can in turn divert candor and invite sidestepping. You may find that the implicit need to maintain proper pause, equanimity, and decorum interferes with your ability to be as forthcoming as you may like. And unlike internal employee/workplace conversations, you are not likely to be as free to say what's on your mind in as natural a fashion as you would be with a coworker or boss.

So while the same main principles apply to client interaction as were true in the previous chapters, learning to have these types of conversations means being slightly more dexterous in how you present information and/or respond to challenging situations. What doesn't change though is that there will be some conversations that should happen, others that shouldn't, and those that can't be avoided, not at any cost, no matter what. Take Shirley, for example.

Shirley's Story

I am a Realtor and dreaded conversations are part of my daily business because each transaction has at least *one* situation that keeps me up at night. These range from admitting I made an error or an omission that affects the transaction, informing my client that the *other* agent made an error or omission that affects the transaction or that the title company did, or the mortgage agent did, and on and on and on it goes. Dreaded conversations can include sensitive financial information, requesting death certificates and copies of divorce decrees, or, these days, delivering the news that, while belongings were being packed into the moving van, a mortgage company withdrew funding and someone is now officially homeless.

Once I had to tell a client that, through no fault of mine, UPS had lost a proceeds check for $168,000. Not only was the check lost, but the title company that could replace the check was closed for a Korean holiday and all the decision makers had flown home to Korea. The moment I realized that the situation was what it was, I called the client and told her the check was lost and that I was arranging for a replacement. So, maybe there are *two* cardinal rules: do it fast and offer a solution. Oh, maybe three. Listen to the tongue lashing until it's through.

I used to worry a lot about *how* to deliver the news but realized slowly that it doesn't really matter, as long as you aren't drunk and you tell the truth. My motto? If you have to eat a live frog, do it fast.

Amen. Love the live frog analogy. She's right. But Shirley also raises another very good point. Lots of times you will get thrashed by clients because they expect you to take it in exchange for whatever went wrong. It's part of the deal—sort of. Implicitly at least, it's the way it is, just another one of those things that comes with the territory. To be clear, though, a thrashing does not equal abuse and should not be justified as such. Venting, yes. You may very well be the subject of a client's temporary frustration, keeping in mind that it was you or your organization that presumably screwed up.

I suppose that makes this the "suck it up" chapter more so than the others because there could be times when you are hindered by a limited number of words due merely to the service nature of client-customer relationships. Whereas everything that came before this was about articulating your thoughts and feelings and putting them into words, client and customer conversations are complicated by the fact that you have to figure out a way to say something while being highly mindful that you don't offend, upset, or permanently alienate the other party.

Money Talks—or Not

At work I sometimes think that money should be the easiest thing to talk about due to the transactional nature of business. But that is often not the case. I'm not sure why. It's just paper, a quantitative measure of value that we swap back and forth. But people have so many associations and beliefs tied to money that their ability to discuss it openly and honestly becomes a sizable if not insurmountable challenge.

Lee's Story

I'm having one right now. A client (who has bounced two checks on me already—but he made good on both of them, including the fees) owes me for one more invoice. This guy is an architect who is in millions of dollars deep on a cool historic renovation project that has shaky financing. He owes everyone and his brother money. Every time I have called him about paying this invoice he gives me an excuse that he can't pay me, and I know it's probably true, in a sense, because his credit line is used up and he's trying to get money from his investors. He keeps putting me off and I really need his payment. I can't stand having to ask someone to pay me what they owe me. Yeccch!

In Lee's case, it's just a matter of saying, "I realize you're going through X, but also need you to know that I am going through Y. What's the solution?" Remind him (or her) of your agreement and then ask again what the solution is. All there is to discuss is how each party will meet the terms. It is not a discussion about any other relationship but yours with him. Don't let digressions into his other matters, vendors, invoices, and obligations muddy the water. You may need to repeat yourself. Don't sweat that. It is a very good example of the squeakiest wheel getting the grease. Keep asking. There is nothing wrong with having the same dreaded conversation over and over and over. Sometimes, that's what it takes to get results.

Money is complicated. But we don't help matters by making conversations about it more complex than they have to be. Even in recent months, what with Wall Street imploding and all, we've heard about more "I lost your money" conversations than anyone cares to think about. As Shirley pointed out, there is no easy way to tell clients that you or your company (or UPS) has lost their money. So in order to make it as painless as possible on yourself and the other person, start with, "I have bad news," and end with, "I'll do everything I can to make it right." Whatever comes in the middle should be short and sweet. Very short and sweet.

Financial, economic, and overall market meltdown notwithstanding, facing clients with bad money news happens under far less dire circumstances than the current global proportions we are experiencing now. For my father it was in his financial services firm when one of his partners, whom he'd known and trusted for years, turned out to be the unscrupulous and unsavory one in the bunch. Oh heck, that's putting it mildly. He was a crook. He robbed my dad blind, leaving him on the hook for a lot of money and having to answer to his clients and explain where it all went.

In a nutshell, what happened was my dad's clients paid premiums into an account established by my dad's firm from which claims for health insurance expenses were paid on behalf of a major insurance company through which my father's firm brokered insurance. Basically this guy, who I'll refer to as Carl, used that money to pay his plumber, his country club fees, and his wife's credit-card bills. I later found out she was technically his sister, too—but like Greg and Marcia, Brady Bunch style. Don't ask. That's another story altogether.

Thank goodness for one thing, though. In addition to his sister/wife, Carl was also sleeping with his assistant, who was the one who tipped off my dad that money was being stolen from the clients' accounts. Apparently it slipped out one night between the sheets. Talk about a sociopath. A real charmer, huh? He's not even fit to go on the Ego Patrol. That's pretty bad. Worse was that he left my father and the remaining partners in the unenviable position of having to tell all the people who put their trust in him and his company that their money was gone. Oh, and also that they weren't actually insured the way they thought they were either.

Well, my dad was one cool cucumber. As the story has been told over and over again, he and one of his partners sat down immediately and met with every single client face-to-face. First he said that there had been a problem with Carl, who was no longer with the company. Then he said that their money was gone because it had been used unethically in a scheme that Carl had concocted. With that he gave his assurances that the company had taken the appropriate measures to protect them from any further damage inflicted by Carl. And lastly he vowed that he would make good on every penny (which he did). Believe it or not, all but one client was understanding and agreed to continue their faith in my father and his partners. The company is still thriving today, more than forty years later.

It was through osmosis, I suspect, that I learned how to think like my dad when it came to sorting out and organizing information. An engineer by trade, he would ask, "What are the givens?" before giving an opinion about what he thought I, or anyone, should do or say. What did become clear to me over time, however, was that there was a great deal of value in taking a methodical approach to having difficult conversations. In other words, take the givens and "chunk" out the information into categories. Drop what you want to say in several clean sections that revolve around the singular points you want to or need to make.

So for my father, his points were simply four.

1. First he said that there had been *a problem* with Carl, who was no longer with the company.
2. Then he said that their *money was gone* because it had been used unethically in a scheme that Carl had concocted.
3. With that he gave *his assurances* that the company had taken the appropriate measures to protect them from any further damage inflicted by Carl.
4. And lastly, he *vowed that he would make good* on every penny (which he did).

Organizing yourself and thoughts this way using clear, tight categories will help you avoid entering a verbal labyrinth where it's easy to get lost and be ineffective.

Just a footnote for dramatic value here. That major insurance company that Carl ripped off? Well, they went on to hire Carl as the head of something knowing full well what he had done. In fact, said major insurance company was the first call and emergency meeting my father assembled. After all, Carl had been stealing money from them, too. No big surprise for anyone, except I guess the major insurance company when it came out that sure enough, Carl had done the same thing to them, too. With much deeper pockets and more money to lose—way more money—they pressed charges and I believe crooked Carl finally went to jail.

Getting Creative

On the other end of the spectrum, in contrast is Diane, who worked in a lingerie department not knowing what to say to a customer in an awkward situation.

Diane's Story

At my first job as a salesgirl selling women's nightgowns in a department store, I had an awkward moment when a man came in and asked me to show him something that ripped off easily. I was flustered and told him that I couldn't recommend anything like that. Then he asked me what I thought was sexy, and I escaped this conversation by saying I like flannel nightgowns. I wasn't comfortable using flirting or suggestive techniques in business, even though I've always understood that sex sells and that my coworkers and supervisors would have tacitly approved anything that created sales.

Hmm. Dodging the question. That could work. But it was an intimates department, so in all fairness to the customer, it wasn't an outrageous question. Nonetheless, in a pinch I like the flannel nightgown comeback. It's funny. It's creative.

And it's one way around having to deal directly with what Diane really thought but didn't feel like she could say.

See, with external conversations like this one it's different than having to face someone with whom you share an employer in common. Diane has no relationship with this customer and will probably never see him again. So she has to deal with facing the awkwardness on the spot more so than having a conversation per se. Discussing *anything* with him in any real sense of the word would be overkill. The question then becomes, "Isn't there a way to keep selling and working in a professional manner without turning off the customer and being true to yourself?" Yes, there is. It basically just means finding a way around it, like Diane did, but that doesn't kill the sale/business at the same time.

One option could be to act contemplative for a moment or so and then enlist the help of another salesperson on the floor. Make it a group conversation by asking what she (or he) thinks, which would enable you to get alternative suggestions and divert the attention away from yourself. You might also try to turn it around and ask the customer himself what he likes and from there make selections for him based on his preferences, not yours. If it were me, I might start asking lots of questions about the girlfriend. You know, change the focus. What's she like? How tall? Blue eyes or brown? Blonde, brunette, or redhead? Again, keep the conversation based on the business at hand. His girlfriend. Her nightie.

So in essence, in lieu of letting it get personal, reinvent the situation so as to remove the need to say anything that spills into uncomfortable territory. In this and similar situations, your safest bet is to not let it become about you.

I had a funny story from my retail days along these lines, too. We had a prostitute who used to come into our store on a regular basis. It was the main floor of a specialty retailer, on which I was a manager of one of the departments. She came in constantly to primp herself using our testers right before her "dates." Everyone was getting really grossed out and the companies were beginning to complain that they couldn't keep up with our "tester requests."

You see, initially the plan was that someone on the selling floor staff would be responsible for following her around and tossing anything she touched into the garbage. But after a while, that tactic could not be sustained. For one, the staff was commissioned and there to sell. So it really wasn't fair to pull them away from opportunities to service legitimate customers. Plus it was expensive throwing away so much full-size product so often.

Aside from that, though, what finally propelled the conversation (if you can call it that) one day was when she came into the store, proceeded to select our most expensive perfume tester, lifted her skirt, sprayed it between her legs, and then took a spritz in her mouth. "That does it," I exclaimed as my entire staff gaped, staring at me slack jawed and expectantly as if to say, "Do something!"

They were right. I had to do something. Other customers had been complaining, and we were officially on an allocation for tester quantities. I walked up to her and gently, in the softest voice I could create, said, "Excuse me, Miss? Might I ask you to stop visiting the store to use our testers? The companies provide them to us so that the customers who would like to make a purchase are given the opportunity to try the product before taking it home." She looked at me and walked out. I never saw her again. My guess is that she ended up at Macy's where she'd get lost in the crowd and mayhem. I know. Ew.

And for more on dealing with gross things, my friend Vincent has a career in the fitness industry that spans years and is filled with story after story about difficult, embarrassing, sometimes hilarious, and often impossible conversations. Because he spends most of his time in gyms, his work environment is primed to present situations that must be brought to light and discussed more so than in most other workplaces. For one, he sees his clients—at least many of them—on a regular basis, and very often that means every day. And two, the nature of exercising is riddled with issues that need to be discussed that would never, ever come up in any other environment. So between the ongoing and repeated contact and the sweating, skin, showering, shorts, and smells that all happen in rather tight quarters, there are inevitably conversations that would be otherwise nonexistent in a more transient, less physically active setting. Vincent explains. . . .

Vincent's Story

It is always the hard knock on your office door that quickly snaps you out of your daydreams and back into reality like a bucket of cold water to your face. I assumed that today was no different. "What now?" I said to myself as I returned from the beach in my imagination to the reality of my desk.

The usual host of issues that occur in a gym may cause some less experienced managers to stress out and some high maintenance customers to lose their cool, but they leave me with a, "Ho hum, what next?" kind of attitude.

Broken treadmill? Check the plug. No toilet paper in one of the stalls? Get a fresh roll out of the closet. No towels? Get a stack from the towel bin. Unhappy client? Let me put a smile on your face! Anything else? All routine and easily solved. Staying ahead of the complaint curve is my forte. Checklists, backup plans, constant walk-throughs. You name it, I've got it covered! I run the tightest ship in the fitness industry.

So, back to that knock on the door. My right-hand manager greets me as I open the door and prepare my game face. "Boss, we have a major problem," she said. Uh-oh—for someone like her to say something like that was enough to scare the light out of me! What is it? We have everything running like a top and all systems are 100 percent foolproof. My perfect world was about to crumble. . . . What can it be!?

"Lay it on me," I say. And like a lamb to slaughter, she grabs my hand and leads me up the stairs to the cardio area of the gym. "Breathe," she says.

Now, I have been in many places around the world and have seen, tasted, and smelled some of the most god-awful things that our planet has to offer, but nothing prepared me for this. I held my nose as I tried to recover from the most foul, disgusting odor that I have ever smelled.

In front of me, there was one man, who will now and forever be known as "Smelly Man," on a treadmill, in an area with many treadmills, designed for many people, by himself, running like the devil himself was chasing him. And Lord, did he smell! Like death. Like a thousand dirty pairs of socks. Like someone who did not wash his clothes or body for a year! It was so bad.

I looked over across the gym and the entire regular crowd was on the other side of the room staring back at me. Huddled together in their respective workout areas, smiling, mocking, arms crossed, and their faces saying, "How are you going to handle this one, wise guy?"

My trusty assistant, loyal and true through the thick and thin, patted me on the back and wished me well. I think her parting words were, "Let me know how it goes so I can let everyone know in the future, OK?" She quickly vanished into the crowd.

Well, if you ever have to have a conversation like this one, let me warn you that the person who is reeking is oblivious. Oblivious to himself and to the three hundred people around him, who are quickly moving farther and farther away. Smelly Man was clearly in his own world. Headset on, watching TV, and running furiously like all of the bulls in Pamplona were after him.

Now, if you have never been in this position before, let me tell you the first thing you want to do. Go back to your office and act like you know exactly what you are going to do. Walk with all of the authority and dignity you can muster. This will allow you to save face later on and give the appearance that, yes, you can handle anything and that you gave it 110 percent.

Next, drink water. Plenty of water. This will compensate for any sudden or increased drop in blood pressure that is about to occur. Finally, breathe (clean air, of course!) and reaffirm several times that everything will be OK. And why not? What's the worst that can happen at this point? I noticed the people in the gym trying to peer in on me in my glass office. I am sure they were wondering how I was going to pull this off without a scene. Time for action.

I gathered up a gym bag, a pair of shorts, and a shirt that I thought would fit Smelly Man. I threw in some socks, a lock, a bottle of water, and a towel. If you are going to give a gift, make it a good one is my philosophy.

As I walked up the stairs, I felt the air leave the gym as if a huge vacuum had been turned on. Except for Smelly Man, the entire gym stopped in mid-rep to watch what was going to happen next.

"Sir? Sir?" I said. Smelly Man was so gone into his smelly world that it took me several attempts to get his attention. Finally, just before I thought I would pass out from the odor, he looked at me and shut off the treadmill. As if I just interrupted a man who was about to enjoy a steak dinner with wine, he said, "*What?*"

I held the bag out in front of him and said, "Here is a gift for you. Clean clothing, a lock, some water, and a towel. We have a great locker room downstairs with showers and soap. And shampoo and deodorant. Would you mind?" And I nodded my head toward the stairs. Smelly Man looked at me like I had lobsters coming out of my ears. My subtle hint, which wasn't really all that subtle, had not worked. Maybe I spoke too fast for him to hear me clearly? So, I repeated myself. This time a little slower. "It's a gift. For you. Clean clothing, a lock, some water, and a towel. We have a locker room. Downstairs. Soap, showers, and soap with water to clean up with."

Smelly Man stared at me for an eternity of seconds. He looked at the bag. He looked at me. Then he looked at the bag again. I knew something was coming, but I didn't know what. Finally, looking me straight in the eye he said, "What are you trying to say?"

Something suddenly came over me. I had no choice. I felt that I had to be as direct as the N train pulling into 42nd Street during rush hour. There was no more time for hints, clues, and beating around the bush. The smell was killing me one breath at a time. So I said, "Your clothes smell and so do you." Smelly Man again looked at the bag and looked back at me. I could not believe what I'd just said and I don't think he did either. I thought I was a goner and prepared to block whatever was going to be thrown at me. Instead, Smelly Man took the bag from my hand and got off the treadmill, but not before uttering, "Go to hell."

To the silent cheers of the gym crowd and with bag in hand, Smelly Man walked into the locker room with his head held high. Out of all the difficult situations that I have ever had in the gym, I'm inclined to believe that this was the one that no one could ever top!

Smelly Man continued to be oblivious and eventually, the episode faded into memory. From time to time, he would acknowledge my presence with but a nod of his head.

A prop! It was brilliant, actually. Vincent used the gift as his conversation aid and starter. Everyone has something that helps make him or her feel comfortable and everyone can have a strategy just as unique. It may just take a little thought and practice to discover what works and what doesn't work for you.

In the next example, Pablo is faced with a bit of an odd request from one of his clients and had to find a way to give them the answer that they didn't want to hear.

Pablo's Story

As an artist, I am known internationally for my drawings, paintings, and sculptures of dancers. I often also get commissions to do nude studies of wives, girlfriends, etc. However, I was once asked by a couple to do a painting of them while having sex. I don't have a lot of lines, but this crossed one of them. The hard part was that they were prominent gallery owners who were showing my work. I stalled an answer for as long as I could. I finally just said that I was uncomfortable with the idea. Our relationship chilled a bit after that, but we still interact professionally.

Right. Exactly. Sometimes the answer may just need to be no. Sometimes what you have to say is not what the other parties want to hear. You're almost always better off leveling with them, giving it to them straight and crossing your fingers that they respect you for it. Most times, most people do. And if they don't, that's their problem. Again, though, it's going to boil down to how you say it.

Stalling is one thing and processing the most effective and appropriate response is another. But regardless of how long it takes you to figure out what your response is going to be, you can't let your clients know you think they are weird. Granted, their request could be considered a bit strange, but they didn't think so. There is therefore no need to sit them down and have a powwow about it. Like the lingerie example, the less you say to explain the "No thank you," the more likely you are to maintain some sort of relationship. And like Pablo, if you salvage the professional part, then you're in very good shape.

Really Bad News

Now, after all is said and done, I should point out that there is bad news and then there is *really bad news*. In talking with people throughout the course of writing this book, two things came up that stopped me in my tracks—conversations that left even me thinking, "Holy cow, how does anyone survive *that*?" I found myself cringing as I listened, heart palpitating and skin crawling, as I tried to fathom how hard it must have been.

The first was a story told to me by a client who learned through a Google search that her surgeon had operated on the wrong foot of another patient, which ultimately resulted in the abrupt ending of that patient's skating career. "Ouch," someone at the table said, "Talk about dreading a conversation!" Here this poor fellow closes his eyes one minute, completely vulnerable and trusting some guy in scrubs with his body, and "*bammo*," the next thing he knows, he wakes up to learn, that his doctor "fixed" the wrong side *and* ended his career. How do you face that person with something of that magnitude? What do you say, "I'll do the other one for free and throw in a shoulder"? I honestly have no idea. I can't imagine. It does help put many of the other conversations we've considered thus far into perspective though, wouldn't you say?

Of course, I would think that any normal person's initial reaction would be to run away and hide. But you can't do that. It wouldn't be right. Or try to get someone else to break the news. But that's not an option either. You own it. There's simply no way out. You have no choice but to face it, say you're sorry, and just deal with feeling really stupid and responsible. What else can you do? In my book, nothing. Nada. Zilch. Suck it up.

The second story came from a colleague who told me of the time that she'd offered to watch her boss's bird while he was on vacation. But while the boss was away, her dog accidentally ate the bird. Oh my gosh, where does one even begin? You can't blame the dog. Well, I guess you can, but the boss didn't trust the bird with the dog, the boss trusted the bird with her employee. And it's not like there is someone like Madoff or the Looney Tune in my dad's office to point the finger at. No, in the end, all you can *really* do is the same thing we've said all long for the other examples. Be straightforward and compassionate and don't belabor the point. It just seems so much harder under circumstances when you are the cause of another person being inflicted with unnecessary pain and so much worse when that person had put his or her explicit trust in you. I guess you take it like a punch to the stomach and let time heal. There's no cushion. No buffer. No fall guy. No excuses. It lands on you. My mother would say, "It builds character." Perhaps she's right, but that is only if you choose to use it as an opportunity that makes you stronger and not a reason to go further underground into denial. *That* makes you weaker.

Meanwhile, the best I can do is liken the humiliation and guilt of this kind to what it feels like having to face the rats in the New York City subways. It makes you sick if you think about it for too long, but you can't make them go away. So we live among them because we have to. Not an easy thing to do, but at the same time, it's the only thing *to* do. The difference is that some people look and see with open eyes and accept the presence of the "rats" while others turn away and freak out. Each is a perfectly legitimate response. It's the outcome you need to worry about though when you choose to close your eyes. You think you're safer if you ignore them, but you're not. Instead you're actually more vulnerable because you can't see when the creepy-crawlers approach and it's then when you are bitten the hardest. Our psychology works the same way. Better to see everything in your purview, even it if makes you squirm, so you can manage and maintain the appropriate relationship to, and distance from, your personal discomfort and fear.

So when life doesn't cooperate, whether it's dealing with the rats or admitting a wrong, do your best to accept that something bad happened to you and move on before it makes you sick. I know, it's easier said than done, but it's a process that has to be given the time and space to play itself out and eventually settle.

Lastly, whether you choose to employ an approach in this book like humor, or props, being blindingly blunt or hedging your bets, blurting it out or loading your guns, making a simple polite request, or asking questions to ease into a conversation, the point is that you need to give some thought to what communication strategy will work best for you and choose a method and style that you'll wear well and suits your style best.

10

Closure

"So many books about 'difficult conversations' are essentially 'how to negotiate' guides" was an interesting piece of feedback I received when embarking on the process of writing this book. It got me thinking—and thinking some more. Immediately it was clear that this book was not that. This book is about saying what must be said and clearing the way to say it, not about getting what you want or preparing for a fight. In fact, quite to the contrary, being able to have effective conversations that successfully communicate difficult workplace issues is to understand that there is nothing to negotiate.

Perhaps it's all in the definition. My definition is that dreading a conversation and surviving its challenges are not the same as being concerned with conflict, confrontation, and persuasion. In my mind's eye they are two separate camps, each with its own distinctive set of "rules," if you will. In other words, the point is not to move someone toward your way of thinking or diffuse his or her volatility but rather to learn to give information that leads to better, more shared understanding and healthier work relationships through communication.

As far as conflict goes, I'm one of those people who thinks misunderstandings, hurt feelings, and confusion are healthy, albeit messy at the same time. Without them, I just don't see any other path to clarity, and without clarity we are without the ability to understand one another.

Now, it already came up briefly in one of the earlier examples, but it's worth mentioning again in closing. There will be conversations that feel as though they must be discussed, when in reality, they don't. There is a big difference between the "do-or-die" conversations and the "I need to get something off my chest" conversations. It's easy to get them confused, but the mere feeling of dread should not be the only indicator, nor should it force words out that aren't ready to be heard, despite the fact that you may feel ready to say them. Silence can indeed at times be golden and timing *is* everything in the situations where you *do* have a choice. If something is bothering you, but voicing it doesn't feel quite right in your gut, wait. Mark my words—the right opportunity will present itself. Remember, it's not just the conversation that can strain a relationship but what it leaves behind as well. So should you feel the need to unload what's on your mind or in your heart, stop, wait, and think about it first. There is nothing worse than a forced conversation that didn't need to be forced.

When the time does come and you find yourself having a conversation that you dread, do yourself and the other person a favor and take a few minutes to consider his or her outlook as much as, if not more than, you've considered your own. Ask yourself what that person might be thinking, or feeling, or afraid of. Consider what information or perspective he or she may have and how it might color or change the information and perspective you have and to what extent. Bear in mind that even though you speak the truth, it doesn't make you "right," because there could feasibly be two truths operating simultaneously. Yours and that of the person to whom you are talking. And therein lies the key challenge to effectively communicating, especially when it comes to the most difficult conversations. If you have the capacity to accept and respect the truth from both sides, even if they vary, you will find yourself way ahead of the curve.

But the "right" truth—the mutual truth, the untainted truth—takes a great deal of effort to see accurately and even more work to communicate clearly. And while it seems like the truth should be the easiest and most obvious thing on earth to find, it can actually be one of the hardest. It's kind of like trying to see a sculpture in a big, undefined blob of clay. Eventually though, by carving away at the mass, the shape emerges and becomes clearer and clearer with every whittle. But no matter how perfect the lines and how articulated the statue might be, it's still hard for some people to appreciate its beauty.

Even so, don't be fooled. Truth is a gift. It's a giving act and it's hard to *do*. People know it when they hear it because it resonates deep within the human core. But dealing with yourself and others at that level takes an enormous amount of courage, integrity, and fortitude. And that's what makes offering the truth a "labor of love." Unfortunately, "the love" is lost on many people and can result in a slap to the face rather than a welcoming set of open arms. That's the other person's problem, though, not yours. He or she is the one who loses. It's a shame. Not everyone wants it and because of that seeking and saying the truth doesn't always help bring people closer together.

Like my dad always used to say, "The truth and aging aren't for sissies, and the truth is, we're all aging." So we end up right back where we started from, facing life's basic challenges. Growing up. Divorcing ego. Finding the truth and using it as a means to connect with others, enrich work, and improve lives. In some cases, that will also mean having to disconnect from certain people, because their truth is denial. And so we say, so be it.

Going forward then, when you do have difficult conversations before you, whether it's one where you have a choice or not, it is therefore up to you to gauge how much honesty the situation can bear. Some people have a very low threshold for the truth, which is just more ego inserting itself between you and them. So you have to decide the extent to which you are willing to engage in the games egos play. Considering there is a very real possibility that you could make more enemies than friends the more forthright you are, it becomes a highly personal choice between how truthful you want to be versus the amount of peace you feel you need to maintain in your interaction with others. Together, each will weigh against, and ultimately determine, the overall quality of your relationships.

Now we all know that people come and go. So too do jobs. But skill strengthening is not dependent on anything or anyone but what you have and exercise inside yourself. Regardless of who is stuck where and on what part of the proverbial path, the best anyone can do for him- or herself is to keep moving and not get stuck, too. Everybody can continue to grow and improve his or her communication skills by finding ways to feel secure and avoiding those people, places, and things that don't. It is a very simple formula, really. If you are secure, you are confident; if you are confident, you won't be afraid to try; and if you are not afraid to try, you will become better, more skilled, *confident,* and expert at the mastery of communication.

So I leave you with this. Someone asked me how this book would translate into one PowerPoint slide. And I said:

- Difficult workplace conversations are not about working it out but about getting it out.
- The art *and* craft of communicating well is being able to say it like it is.
- Bite the bullet and just do it.
- Get over the fear so that you can get the conversation over with.
- All you can do is what you can do, but at least you can do it well.
- Telling someone the truth is a giving act and one to be proud of.
- Life is what you make it.
- Ego will kill the spirit of healthy, human conversations.

Part 3

The How

11

Dreaded Conversations in Action

So, what does all this mean in real life and in real time in the real world of work? Well, for one, it means adopting some key phrases and rules of thumb not only to help launch your dreaded conversations but also to guide you through the dialogue in the most effective way. Eventually, you are likely to gravitate toward certain words or combinations of words simply because some will work better with your personality and in the context of the particular relationship than others. The point is to remember that one of the biggest facilitators to a successful conversation is your own sense of ease, because if you are comfortable, the chances increase exponentially that the other person will be, too—and vice versa.

In the pages that follow, I offer some examples of potential workplace conversations, scripted and followed by callouts of helpful wording and phrasing as well as possible conversation starters. Keep in mind that part of the goal of getting the conversation going is that you establish either what you want, where it's going, or what it's about.

Also, because there are generally certain things that are good to say and others that aren't so good, I'll highlight them as well as each conversation moves along. In all, remember, there is a point to be made that needs to be clear but that will also most likely require a little finessing somewhere and somehow.

SCENARIO 1
Employee to Boss: I Want to Be Promoted

An employee is afraid to approach her boss about her desire to discuss a career path, fearing that she will be looked down upon for appearing to have her eye on advancement when people are dropping like flies in round after round of layoffs.

> **Employee:** Can I schedule some time to talk with you?
> **Boss:** About what?
> **Employee:** My performance . . . you know, how I'm doing.
> **Boss:** Sure, let's talk now.
> **Employee:** OK. Thank you.
> *[Awkward silence]*

Employee: Well, basically I just wanted to get your thoughts about how I'm doing and where you think there may be opportunities for me to learn, because ultimately my goal is to keep growing. I'm clear this is a bad time but felt it was worth us connecting on my performance anyway. I'd also love to get your advice as to where you think I belong. What would you suggest I do?

[Boss invariably gives feedback and observations about job performance.]

Employee: Is there anything you would suggest now that I should be doing to prepare me for later?

[Boss will give more advice. Then it's the employee's turn to offer her thoughts and express her interests.]

Employee: Well, I enjoy X and am interested in the business part of the industry, so if you think there are opportunities for me to help out where I could learn, I'd love the chance to try. And would you say that we could touch base again sometime in the next quarter to make sure that I'm on the right track?

Boss will say yes, but even if the manager wasn't inclined to discuss her career path, the conversation should still follow the same format:

1. Find out how you're doing.
2. Ask what you need to do to improve your standing.
3. *Then* express what you want and are hoping to accomplish.

The Breakdown

- **Start** by establishing that you would like to have a conversation, but respect whatever demands and restrictions may be on your boss and his or her schedule.
- **Good things to say:** "I want to learn." "I want to grow." "I want to contribute."
- **Bad things to say:** "I deserve it." "You owe me." "I work harder than anyone else."
- **Do** get a reality check first on how you're doing. Ask for advice on how to move forward, and then make your aspirations clear.
- **Don't** jump into the conversation and immediately make it all about you and what you want.
- **Tip:** Use questions to prompt a conversation in order to understand what the other person is thinking.

SCENARIO 2

Employee to Boss: Sorry, No Can Do

An employee is torn when his boss asks him to lie to a client by fudging test scores of an incoming candidate in order to make the candidate look better on paper than she actually is. He does not want to do it.

> **Employee:** With all due respect, sir, I'd prefer that you make the adjustments to the test. I'm not comfortable with it.
> **Boss:** Why not?

Employee: Well, because technically, it's not true.
We'd be giving the client false information, which is
totally fine if that's the direction you want to take this,
but I'd appreciate it if you'd respect my feelings about it.
Boss: I didn't ask you to tell me what you thought.
I asked you to change the test scores.
Employee: Yes, sir, I understand, but perhaps we
just have different definitions here. I have a very
good relationship with this client, and I don't want
to do anything to damage it. It they found out, that
wouldn't be good for our business at all. It's really not
a good position for me, or any of us, to be in.
Boss: How would they find out?
Employee: Well, for one, the candidate may not
actually be able to perform, which will raise the
question right away. What if we gave her a chance
to retest? Maybe her scores will improve in their
own right. Then no one has to be in the position of
bending the truth. Otherwise, I just don't have it in
me. I'm sorry.

The Breakdown

- **Start** by establishing that you do not want to do it.
- **Good things to say:** "I'm sorry." "I'm uncomfortable." "It's not who I am." "I'll pass." "With all due
  respect, I need/would like to decline."
- **Bad things to say:** "I can't believe you'd suggest I stoop
  so low." "That's unethical." "You're wrong to ask me."
  "How dare you ask me to do something so sleazy?"

- **Do** stay on point.
- **Don't** make judgmental statements or let it become a debate about morals.
- **Tip:** Make a sound, solid argument, offer solutions or alternatives, and stick to your guns if you don't feel right about it.

SCENARIO 3

Employee to Boss: I Deserve an Increase

An employee is asked to take on extra responsibilities in the absence of a coworker who resigned. The company decides not to fill the position, so in turn the employee is left doing the work of two people, if not more. He feels he deserves to be compensated for his additional efforts and time put in. After wrestling with feeling taken advantage of, he finally works up the courage to confront his boss.

> **Employee [to boss]:** Do you have a second?
> **Boss:** I will in twenty minutes. Come back then and I'll have time.
> *[Twenty minutes later]*
> **Boss:** So what's up?
> **Employee:** Well, I've been thinking. Something has been on my mind lately, and it's bothering me. It's not easy for me to bring up, but I have to.
> **Boss:** What is it?
> **Employee:** It's the way my job has changed since X left. I respect that the opening is not being filled and

that there are reasons for that, but in the meantime,
I've picked up the additional work, which has
fundamentally changed the nature of my job, not to
mention the volume of my workload. So I wanted to
ask you if you were at all open to adjusting my salary
to reflect that.

The boss will say either yes or no. You can't control his
or her answer because there is an inordinate amount of contextual organizational information to which you will not be
privy. It is information that affects a manager's ability to issue
increases or not. So the best you can do is ask the question
and do it professionally and skillfully so that if the answer is
no, you've left it on a positive note and set up a pathway to
revisit the subject again at a later date. In the meantime, you
will have a very clear picture of where you stand and can use
the time to hone in on what you need to do to make yourself
more valuable and increase your chances for success down
the road. Sometimes the bigger factor that weighs in on these
situations is not what you say but the timing of when you
say it.

The Breakdown

- **Start** by establishing that something is troubling you.
- **Good things to say:** "I was wondering if you were
  open to . . ." "I'd like to see what you think about . . ."
  "I wanted to get your thoughts about the feasibility
  of . . ."
- **Bad things to say:** "More work means more pay." "I
  work twice as hard and should be paid twice as much."

- **Do** gently pose the question.
- **Don't** demand anything or try to negotiate.
- **Tip:** Your tone needs to be very conversational or you run the risk of turning your boss off, which tarnishes future discussions about this and other topics.

SCENARIO 4

Employee to Boss: I'd Like a Raise

An employee has been working at the same rate for three years and feels he or she deserves a raise.

> **Employee:** May I ask you a question?
> **Boss:** You may.
> **Employee:** First, let me say that I really like it here. In the last three years I've enjoyed my job and been very happy. The only thing that I'm struggling with is the fact that my salary has not changed. So, I guess the first thing I need to know is whether you are satisfied with my performance, and then, if you are, if we could talk about the possibility of planning an increase in my pay.
> *[Again, the boss will either respond with a yes or no. If it's a no, then continue.]*
> **Employee:** Just so I'm clear then, would you mind telling me how the pay system works? At a minimum I'd like to understand it so that I can make whatever adjustments I may need to make on my end.

The Breakdown

- **Start** by establishing that you are happy so as to mitigate the chances that you will be perceived as a complainer.
- **Good things to say:** "Are you open to it?" "Can we discuss it?" "What can I do?"
- **Bad things to say:** "I've waited too long." "I deserve it." "I make less than everyone else." "It's not fair."
- **Do** express your willingness to learn and desire to understand.
- **Don't** make threats or give ultimatums.
- **Tip:** It is critical to confirm that your boss is satisfied with your performance because if he or she is not, that will be the reason you are told for not getting a raise.

SCENARIO 5
Employee to Boss: I'm Resigning

An employee has been with her company since she graduated from high school. She started in the mailroom and rose through the ranks into a management job. She feels a great sense of loyalty because the company paid for her college tuition, sponsored her through the immigration process so that she would be "legal," and gave her flexible work arrangements when she wanted to have children. But now she is no longer happy in her job and wants to leave. She feels torn and conflicted and can't imagine how to break the news.

Employee: I don't even know where to begin here. This is unbelievably hard for me. I have been going through some changes when it comes to my career and find that I am feeling unfulfilled as of late. I have been here my whole life and am appreciative beyond words—everyone here has been so good to me—but I'm just not happy anymore. I'd like to move on to something else outside of this organization. I feel as though I need exposure to things I don't know as well so that I can continue to grow and be challenged. I'll do whatever you need from me to make the transition work and will work within a time frame that you're comfortable with. But mostly, I'll be forever grateful.

The Breakdown

- **Start** by establishing that you are human, struggling, and grateful.
- **Good things to say:** "Thank you." "I need to move on." "I want to be challenged." "I want to learn something new." "I'd like to keep growing and expanding my skills."
- **Bad things to say:** "There is nothing here for me anymore." "I'm bored." "I need something better."
- **Do** make it clear how much you appreciate your growth and experience *but* that it no longer offers you the opportunities you need to keep expanding yourself.
- **Don't** put down the company in any way in your attempt to say that it's not good enough an environment for you.
- **Tip:** Speak from your heart.

Scenario 6

Employee to Boss: Let Me Give You Some Advice

An "older worker" reports to a very young boss who has virtually no experience. To compensate for her shortcomings, the boss barks orders at employees and takes shortcuts to cover up her mistakes. She also has a tendency to blame her underlings for her screw-ups. The "mature" employee, who has been a manager himself, is frustrated because he knows how to make the team run more efficiently and effectively due to his years of experience in business.

> **Employee:** If I may, with all due respect, I feel that there are some things we can do and/or talk about that could improve not only our relationship but the relationships of everyone on the team.
>
> **Boss:** What do you mean? What's wrong with our relationship?
>
> **Employee:** Well, I don't think we interact in the most productive way possible.
>
> **Boss:** I have no problem with you.
>
> **Employee:** Thank you. And I appreciate that, but I think that there are times when we could do a better job at communicating with one another.
>
> **Boss:** Like what?
>
> **Employee:** Well, I think there is some value to getting input from others and drawing from their various experiences. It seems as though we sometimes have tension here because things get rushed and it

occasionally shows up in how you respond. Our exchanges can be too short and abrupt for us to be effective. So, might I suggest that you take advantage of me more and use me for my skills? I'm here to help the cause, not hinder it.

The Breakdown

- **Start** by establishing that you respect her position.
- **Good things to say:** "We're in this together." "What can I do to help improve communication and slow things down?" "Use me for what experience I have."
- **Bad things to say:** "You have no idea what you're doing." "You're barely old enough to be my daughter." "You should be working for me."
- **Do** make it clear that your main interest or objective in having the conversation is to improve the relationship so that everyone, including your boss, performs at a higher level.
- **Don't** throw age and experience in her face. It will only make her feel more insecure.
- **Tip:** Make the whole tone of the conversation "we." Overall, it should be positioned as a move toward the "greater good," which means the goals and objectives of the organization, which she is expected to carry out. Just be careful not to start speaking for other people on the team. When it comes down to it, the dialogue is between the two of you and no one else. That focus and discipline are how relationships become strengthened.

SCENARIO 7

Boss to Employee: You Are Out of Line

An employee mouths off at his boss in front of a customer, which is the final straw after a series of combative outbursts in meetings.

> **Boss:** We need to talk. Let's go into my office.
>
> **Employee:** What's up?
>
> **Boss:** The hostility and aggression in your behavior has to stop. You've directed it toward me and others and it's a problem.
>
> **Employee:** What? I'm not hostile.
>
> **Boss:** I'm afraid you are. Today when you blew up in front of the client and made negative comments about our company, it was totally inappropriate and reflects extremely poorly on you and your professionalism.
>
> **Employee:** But I wasn't . . .
>
> **Boss:** Look, we're not going to debate this and I'm not going to sit here to try to get you to see yourself. I am here to tell you that your behavior in that situation and recent meetings is unacceptable here. I won't tolerate it.

The Breakdown

- **Start** by establishing that there is a problem right up front, and make sure you go somewhere private to discuss it.

- **Good things to say:** "You're out of line." "That was out of bounds." "Not cool." "Not good." "Unacceptable."
- **Bad things to say:** "I assume you know why we're here." "You've got some serious anger issues." "Everyone is pissed off at you."
- **Do** hit the point hard and be explicitly clear about where you *and* the other person stand.
- **Don't** argue about what you observed and try to justify its validity, and don't ever make the person feel ganged up on by saying, "Everyone else thinks so."
- **Tip:** Avoid making it a personal attack or drawing conclusions about one's emotions. Instead, after you have made your point, explore whether there might be a reasonable explanation that provides insight into the behavior. You need to know and you also may learn that there is an easy "fix."

Scenario 8

Boss to Employee: We Have a Problem

An employee in excellent standing has her first child, who ends up being constantly sick, resulting in the mother/employee being out of work a lot. This puts a strain on her job and affects her ability to be effective. She needs to be made aware that her daughter's health is adversely affecting her performance and the organization.

> **Employee:** I can't come in tomorrow. "Baby" is sick again.

Boss: OK, now we have to talk. This has become a problem. Something has got to give here. You know I think you are terrific and that you are one of my best employees, but you can only be so good if you're not here to do what needs to be done.

Employee: Well, she's sick. I don't know what else to say. It's just the way it is. She's my responsibility.

Boss: I understand that, but so is this. It's been going on for a long time, and like I say all the time about a lot of things, "It's OK until it's not OK," and it's not OK anymore.

Employee: But what do you want me to do? She's just a baby.

Boss: I can't answer that for you. You have to figure it out. But somehow you need to have a contingency plan if she gets sick, because this is not working. Maybe work the weekend, get a babysitter? I don't know.

Employee: That's not going to fly.

Boss: OK, well this is not flying either, which is what I need you to understand. I realize it's not your fault and that she is just an innocent little baby who didn't ask to get sick all the time, but you're not seeing the big picture here and how your situation is affecting the other people involved. By thinking it's OK, you're putting us in a really crummy position. I want to work with you and I want us to find a solution, so can you think about how we might resolve this and let me know tomorrow what you come up with?

The Breakdown

- **Start** by establishing how valued a worker the employee is, but that her contribution doesn't make her immune from the feedback if she is unable to do her job.
- **Good things to say:** "We need a solution." "You're not taking everyone into consideration." "Our relationship has become imbalanced as a result of this."
- **Bad things to say:** "It's your problem." "Not my problem/responsibility." "You're the one who decided to have a baby." "I've put up with it long enough."
- **Do** work together toward a solution.
- **Don't** throw up your hands in despair and say something stupid that you'll regret.
- **Tip:** Remember that it is no one's fault. It's just a situation that needs to be resolved and that requires all parties to be calm, cool, thoughtful, and probably creative.

SCENARIO 9

Boss to Employee: You're No Longer Employed

A company is making cuts, and an employee who does not have any performance issues must be let go.

> **Boss:** I have bad news. I'm sorry to have to tell you this, but as a result of the recent changes to the organization, your job is being cut.

[It is good to give some contextual information here; for example:
- *In an effort to create more efficiency, we are combining departments.*
- *The organization has imposed a strategic initiative to reduce headcount by 25 percent.*
- *The department is being moved to another state where we already have staff.]*

Employee: But why me and not someone else?

Boss: Because it's about the job, not you. It's the relationship of your role to the organization that made it vulnerable. I understand how you feel. It's perfectly natural.

[Sit calmly and quietly through the reaction.]

Boss: So let's talk about what I can do to help *[e.g., call relatives, get a soda, sit outside, plan next steps, outsourcing services, whatever]*, part of which means getting you prepared for the transition out and taking you through the exit process.

The Breakdown

- **Start** by establishing that you have bad news.
- **Good things to say:** "I'm sorry." "It's organizational, not personal."
- **Bad things to say:** "You're fired." "It's not my fault."
- **Do** get right to the point.
- **Don't** make small talk and pussyfoot around.
- **Tip:** Keep the focus on the fact that it's the role that has been deemed no longer necessary, *not* the person.

SCENARIO 10

Boss to Employee: You're Not Cutting It

An employee is not performing to meet expectations, and her manager is breaking the news to her for the first time.

> **Boss:** We have a situation here that we need to rectify.
> **Employee:** Like what?
> **Boss:** There are issues with your performance. You are not meeting expectations.
> **Employee:** How come you haven't told me before?
> **Boss:** I'm telling you now. Here's what is wrong . . . *[Give details.]*
> **Employee:** But everyone does that . . .
> **Boss:** This is not about anyone else. I am having the conversation with you. I'm not here to argue, I'm here to give you the information you need to improve. If you choose not to take it, then this could turn into a termination conversation. It's up to you.

The Breakdown

- **Start** by establishing that there is a problem.
- **Good things to say:** "What you are doing is not working." "We need to figure this out in order for you to succeed here."
- **Bad things to say:** "I've had it with you." "Your value here is waning." "You're wasting my time."
- **Do** be explicitly clear about the problems with performance, including specific examples and their impact on the team and/or organization.

- **Don't** get into an argument or start justifying your position. Just keep saying it like it is and bringing him or her back to the issue or issues at hand—which is whatever he or she is doing wrong.
- **Tip:** It is common for employees in this situation to stray from the topic. Keep bringing it back to the fact the conversation is between the two of you and does not pertain to anyone or anything else.

Note: Say this employee were *not* to improve. If this were a termination conversation, it would be similar in nature. You would just have to insert something along the lines of the following:

- "It's time for us to part company. This job and/or this company is not bringing out the best in you."
- "Therefore, your employment with us will end on *[date]*."
- "We need to separate so that you can find a better place/ fit that works for you."
- "This is not working out. I need to let you go."

SCENARIO 11
Boss to Employee: Sorry, It's Just Not the Right Fit

An employee, through no fault of his own, is just not getting it. He requires a great deal of oversight, which consumes too much of his manager's time. It's not that he is a poor worker or unwilling to try. Rather, it's just that he requires too much attention and oversight, which burdens his manager and hinders her ability to get her job done well, too. She has become weary trying to "get him there" and therefore has to let him go.

> **Boss:** Gosh, this is tough for me, but it has to be said. I know we've been working a lot together on your development, and while I do enjoy working with you, I'm just not seeing the results. We've tried and tried lots of different things, and without seeing any movement forward, I just don't think this is the right fit for you. It wasn't easy, but I've come to the determination that we've given it enough time and it's just not working. So, we need to part company, which I'm hoping will free you up to pursue a role more conducive to your strengths. I will help you in any way that I can and am very sorry that it didn't work out.

The Breakdown

- **Start** by establishing that you feel bad about the outcome.
- **Good things to say:** "It's no one's fault, just not the right chemistry." "If it's not working, it's better to figure out what does."
- **Bad things to say:** "I've tried everything." "You just don't get it." "Let's end this and put you out of your misery."
- **Do** make it more about the fit than about the individual's ability or performance.

- **Don't** rehash everything you've done to remedy the situation. It will just make the person feel worse.
- **Tip:** It is sometimes helpful to think about situations like this one as similar to ending any other kind of relationship. While it can be painful, staying together when it's not right does no one any good either.

SCENARIO 12

Boss to Employee: Now, You're Fired

After multiple warnings, no improvement, and the continuation of a bad attitude, a manager has no choice but to terminate an employee.

> **Boss:** OK, so we've now been down this road a few times, and frankly I'm just not seeing any change. You've had ample opportunities to turn things around, and for whatever reason, you have not been able to. So as it was stated in your last three warnings, you were prepared that this would be our final discussion, which makes today your last day of employment here. Are you more comfortable retrieving your belongings, or would you like me to do it for you?

The Breakdown

- **Start** by establishing that this is not new, but rather a follow-up on many conversations that came before.
- **Good things to say:** "There's no point in dragging this out." "Based on our numerous discussions regard-

ing your performance, this should not be coming as a surprise to you." "I'm sorry, but this is the way it unfolded."

- **Bad things to say:** "You had your chance." "It wasn't my idea."
- **Do** own what you have to say.
- **Don't** get sidetracked.
- **Tip:** It is usually said to be most advantageous to conduct terminations on Mondays or Fridays. But here is what I learned by engaging in the debate about which day is the best day to fire someone:

  Creative industries tend to attract "sensitives," people who are more apt to feel their emotions on the spot than those individuals found in the "harder industries," such as finance and law. Generally speaking, Fridays work well for sensitives because they then have the weekend to receive support from friends and family. Their first inclination is to want to process the shock, disappointment, or discomfort by working it out/talking it out.

  However, on the other hand, the competitive, type A, go-go-go types tend to prefer getting the axe on a Monday because they feel more productive when they can get up the next morning, hit the phones, and start working their contacts to set up interviews ASAP.

  Needless to say, these are extremely loose observations, for which I have no scientific evidence whatsoever, other than the anecdotal data I've accumulated over the years. Food for thought anyway, at the very least.

Scenario 13
Boss to Employee: We're Being Downsized

A company has been restructured, and, as a result, a manager has to eliminate two of the people on his ten-person team.

> **Boss:** I have bad news. The company has been given a directive to reduce the workforce by 20 percent. Unfortunately, because your performance reviews rank you in the lowest tier, or bottom 20 percent, performance-wise, I need to let you go. I'm sorry.

The Breakdown

- **Start** by establishing that it is not going to be an easy or pleasant conversation.
- **Good things to say:** "I wish you well." "Do you have any questions?"
- **Bad things to say:** "We are cutting out the dead weight." "You're fired."
- **Do** bite the bullet and get right to the point.
- **Don't** beat around the bush.
- **Tip:** Using numbers and, more specifically, percentages is a useful and effective way to soften the blow. Normally people don't appreciate feeling like numbers, but in this case, they create a little distance and help the employee save face. In other words, it becomes an equation, not a personal reflection.

SCENARIO 14

Boss to Employees: Your Jobs Have Been Eliminated

An entire department is being cut and phased out because it is antiquated and a new, more modern department is being created to replace it. None of the workers in the old department have the skills needed to work in the new one.

> **Boss:** I have sad news. Our department has been undergoing a fair amount of scrutiny lately in an effort to understand its value to the company. An evaluation was intended to assess just how slow our processes were and how dated our systems have become. After much analysis, the decision was made to do away with our function entirely and outsource it to people who have the skills needed to bring us into the twenty-first century.
>
> **Employee:** So why don't you train us to be able to be useful in a new capacity?
>
> **Boss:** Because we are past that. We are draining the company's resources, and it's not good for the business.
>
> **Employee:** But that's not fair.
>
> **Boss:** Look, this is so not about being fair. Things change. They live, they die. We have become extinct in the context of this organization. It's time to move on.

The Breakdown

- **Start** by establishing the context of the situation.
- **Good things to say:** "It is what it is and there is nothing we can do about it." "We are a casualty of progress."

- **Bad things to say:** "This company sucks." "We weren't appreciated."
- **Do** lay it on the line.
- **Don't** bad-mouth the company or be negative in any way.
- **Tip:** Provide as many details as possible. People will feel anxious, so the more information you give, the less uncertain they will feel and the more at ease they will be.

SCENARIO 15
Boss to Employees: We're Closing

A company is closing its doors, and each manager has to let his or her employees know before the news "hits the streets."

> **Boss:** This is not going to be pleasant, but you need to know before it goes public. We have not been able to sustain our business, and the decision has been made to shut the company down in a systematic and orderly way so as to avoid an unmanageable collapse. We want to have the time to talk with each employee personally, which is why we are sitting here together now. Each group will be phased out gradually. Our last day of operation will be six weeks from today.

The Breakdown

- **Start** by establishing that it is going to be a difficult conversation.

- **Good things to say:** "Unfortunately, we didn't make it." "We're all in this together." "We'll get through it."
- **Bad things to say:** "If it hadn't been for that new CEO, we'd be fine." "I don't what to tell you." "Suck it up."
- **Do** allow any humanistic feelings to show through.
- **Don't** blame someone else for the failure. It is unlikely that you can know for sure what *actually* happened. There's no point.
- **Tip:** Avoid trying to fill the space and time with empty words.

SCENARIO 16

Coworker to Coworker: You Did What?

A coworker confided to another coworker on e-mail that he hacked into their boss's computer and stole highly confidential information.

> **Coworker 1:** We need to talk. I've been giving some thought to what you told me earlier.
> **Coworker 2:** Yeah?
> **Coworker 1:** I have a problem with it.
> **Coworker 2:** But *you* didn't do anything wrong.
> **Coworker 1:** But now I know, and I'm really uncomfortable with it. You know as well as I do that the company has security rules about any kind of breach. By just telling me and making me aware, you put me at risk and we could both get fired.
> **Coworker 2:** We're not going to be fired.

Coworker 1: But that's not the point. I agreed not only to *not* do something like that but to disclose it if I became aware of it.

Coworker 2: You're overreacting.

Coworker 1: Well, that may be the case, but it doesn't change the fact that I am now in this position that I don't want to be in.

Coworker 2: So what are you going to do?

Coworker 1: I'm going to ask you to figure out a way to fix it or I'll have no choice.

Coworker 2: You mean you'd rat me out?

Coworker 1: Are you kidding me? First, you shouldn't have done it, and, second, you shouldn't have told me. What did you expect?

The Breakdown

- **Start** by establishing that you have something important on your mind that you have to say.
- **Good things to say:** "It is unreasonable to expect me to conceal this." "It is of your doing." "The responsibility of this should not be in my lap."
- **Bad things to say:** "You're a liar." "You're a cheat." "How stupid could you be?"
- **Do** soften the threat to expose by giving the person a chance to come clean (or come up with a story) his or her own way.
- **Don't** fall for tattletale manipulation.
- **Tip:** It's not about the person, it's about the situation. It doesn't matter why it happened or what personal quality it may reflect. It's about how you feel being put in that position.

SCENARIO 17

Coworker to Coworker: About Last Night

One employee makes a blatant (and sloppy) pass at another employee during a company picnic after becoming completely inebriated. They sit near each other at work but don't actually know one another very well. It's the next morning, and she has to face him.

> **She says:** Ahem.
> *[He looks up and smiles awkwardly. She's blushing.]*
> **He says:** Hey.
> **She says:** Hey. Can I talk to you privately for a sec?
> **He says:** Sure.
> *[They go into a nearby conference room.]*
> **She says:** I'm so absolutely horrified.
> *[He says nothing.]*
> **She says:** Look, I know I don't know you well at all, and I'm so sorry I came on to you the way I did yesterday. It was stupid. I shouldn't have had so much to drink.
> **He says:** Ya think? Look, it's fine.
> **She says:** Oh wow, thank you for being so cool about it. Does everyone else think I'm a complete ass now, too?
> **He says:** The truth? Um, pretty much, yes.
> **She says:** Damn. I guess I'll just have to wait it out. Eventually they'll forget. They have to . . . I hope.
> **He says:** Yup, until the next person does it.

She says: Well again, please accept my apology.
I don't know what else to say except I am so
embarrassed and regret putting you in that position.

The Breakdown

- **Start** by establishing that you have appalled yourself
  with your own behavior.
- **Good things to say:** "I apologize." "I was wrong."
  "I messed up." "I showed extremely poor judgment."
- **Bad things to say:** "But you looked so hot." "I couldn't
  control myself." "I couldn't help it."
- **Do** keep it clean.
- **Don't** make excuses.
- **Tip:** You can't undo a situation like this one, so don't try.
  Acknowledge it, say you're sorry, and forget about it.

SCENARIO 18

Employee to Client: I Have Really Bad News

An employee is working on a project for a major client and
was in charge of transporting files that were highly confidential trade secrets. But the employee made a stop on the way
home to meet another client for drinks and left behind the
briefcase containing the sensitive files.

Employee: This is very difficult for me to tell you.
Client: What happened?

Employee: I lost the files that I was in charge of.

Client: You what? You can't be serious! Do you have any idea . . .?

[Screaming, furious, scathing expletives fly.]

Employee: I'm so sorry. I understand how bad this is.

Client: The hell you do! If you had any clue, you wouldn't have let it happen.

Employee: Look, I messed up. I know it. I'm sorry. What can I do to rectify it?

Client: Are you joking? You can't fix this.

Employee: No I can't, not exactly, but for what it's worth, I don't want our relationship to end over this either, although I would certainly understand you feeling the need to give us the axe. We do have a history of producing results for you and providing excellent service here, which I might add, you've been extremely pleased with.

Client: Yeah, until this happened.

Employee: Understood, but emotions are high. I would only ask that we can talk about it at a later date when we are both calmer.

The Breakdown

- **Start** by establishing that this is not going to be an easy conversation.
- **Good things to say:** "I have bad news." "I'm sorry." "I understand." "I'll do whatever is necessary to make it right."

- **Bad things to say:** "You shouldn't have given me something if it was so sensitive" (even though that might be true). "It wasn't my fault." "I lost my bearings because I drank too much."
- **Do** apologize profusely and take the heat until it becomes unreasonable, at which point you should suggest reconvening under less volatile circumstances.
- **Don't** stick around for an emotional beating if it becomes abusive. Venting is one thing, but being a verbal punching bag is quite another.

Note: Now if this conversation were to take place with an angry boss, it would be very similar. You could borrow the same structure, approach, and verbiage and attempt to handle it the same way.

Scenario 19
Employee to Client: You Have to Pay Me/Us for That

A client starts adding more work to a project after it is already under way without discussing appropriate compensation for changing the scope of the job.

> **Employee/Contractor/Consultant:** Unfortunately, there isn't room in our agreement to accommodate this extra work, but I'm happy to draw up a secondary proposal to give you an idea of what it would cost.

The Breakdown

- **Start** by establishing that an agreement exists, which should presumably provide some clarity on the scope of the job.
- **Good things to say:** "Let's back up and redefine the scope." "I was not aware that our agreement included that . . ."
- **Bad things to say:** "I didn't agree to that." "You never said you wanted that." "There is money involved here."
- **Do** respond in an easy and casual way as if it's no big deal.
- **Don't** avoid it. It's a slippery slope.
- **Tip:** Make it more about your desire to "give" than about your desire to "take."

SCENARIO 20

Employee to Client: You're Fired

A client is deemed to be too difficult after much servicing, coddling, and attention. The client/company consists of an abusive and disrespectful bunch of executives who change their minds and direction and take advantage of their vendor's good nature. An employee of the vendor has to deliver the news that his company has decided that this one client is simply not worth the aggravation, even though it is a substantial source of revenue.

> **Employee:** We need to have a conversation.
> **Client:** Go ahead.

Employee: Over the time that we've been working together, we've run into some roadblocks, some of which we've been able to overcome better than others. But overall, this relationship is a difficult one for us, and it's not something we feel comfortable continuing to engage in. We would like to terminate/not renew our agreement and go our separate ways.

Client: What exactly have we done that makes us so horrible?

Employee: I'm not saying you are horrible. No, not at all. Please don't misunderstand what I am saying. It's just that your style of working is not in accord with our style. That's all. We're just not in sync. My guess is that there is probably another company out there who is better suited to meet your needs than we are. In the meantime, we do very much appreciate the opportunity we've had to work with you and hope you'll continue to gain the benefits of the services we've provided.

The Breakdown

- **Start** by establishing that all is not well on the western front.
- **Good things to say:** "No harm, no foul." "We're not right for you."
- **Bad things to say:** "You are the worst client we've ever had." "You're a bunch of animals."
- **Do** remain calm and deliberate. Exit gracefully.
- **Don't** let emotions take the conversation into a different direction, and don't list all of their faults. It's not your place or your job to clue them in.

- **Tip:** Conversations may ensue that develop from the initial conversation itself. Allow them to happen. Great and valuable revelations may emerge.

After reading each of these hypothetical conversations, you may have found them to be alike in certain ways. That's because they are. Generally speaking, they all flow through a similar nuts-and-bolts approach, which calls for being direct at the entry point and attempting to say it like it is in the most authentic way possible. Frankly, they remind me of those *Mad Libs* games where you just fill in different words over a basic underlying structure that remains intact. That's all it is really. There is no need to overanalyze it. To wrap up the points I've made over and over *and over* in this book: all that thinking in your head only leads to a lack of action in your mouth.

You may also have noticed that the tips, dos, don'ts, and good versus bad things to say are interchangeable in many cases, particularly within like sections. That's true, too, although naturally, each person conducting the conversation will have to take the core conversational guts that I put forth and sandwich them between his or her own heart words, combined with language that is appropriate for the individual personalities, egos, situations, organizations, and relationships involved.

See, the thing to remember is that employment is a two-way street. Each side has a point of view that needs to be seen and understood by the other. Your goal is to first get in the shoes of the other person and acknowledge where he or she stands. Then, when it's your turn to elucidate your own position or perspective, you can attempt to balance both. *That* is what makes a good communicator. For that matter, it's also what makes for a healthy relationship and positive work environment. As soon as things tilt too far to one side, the chance to create a harmonious and positive outcome becomes hindered and you become handicapped in your ability to produce the results you want.

Accomplishing this effort of balancing your needs with the needs of others, however, assumes that each individual can articulate his or her own point of view. But that is not always possible because of many of the reasons we've already discussed. It is very hard to know what to say in the first place, if you haven't spent some time trying to also know how you feel. It's this disconnect between cognition and emotion that I believe causes so much inherent angst for people when it comes to communication. And while this entire book has been about getting over (and through) "the conversation" itself, wouldn't it be nice if we could also relieve the stress and dread that precedes it?

Well, we can try. So I say sort yourself out beforehand. In other words, if you give yourself some space to process your own thoughts and feelings, you can then start to rehearse how they might exit your mouth in the form of words. Doing this is a much more productive use of your time and energy than to race and obsess about how much you're dreading facing the person with what you have to say.

On the other hand, if you deny yourself a process and choose to wait until the actual conversation is under way, you're stuck with your head trying to think while your heart is trying to feel and your mouth is trying to talk. That is as hard to coordinate on the spot as trying to rub your belly, pat your head, and sing a song all at the same time, which, as those of us who may have ever tried are well aware, is no easy task. So forge ahead. There is nothing to fear and nothing to dread. But be sure to remember that what you really become when you master the art of difficult conversations is much more than a good communicator. You become a strategist, analyst, and humanitarian who knows how to weigh a situation, understand the players, and evaluate the circumstances in order to move yourself, your relationships, and your organization forward by simply talking sensibly and with compassion. And imagine—you won't lose a wink of sleep!

Index